IMAGES
of America

VIRGINIA BEACH
JEWEL RESORT
OF THE ATLANTIC

And the ambitious vine,
Crowns with his purple mass
       The cedars reaching high
       To kiss the sky,
The cypress, pine,
And useful sassafras.

And cheerfully at sea,
Success you still entice,
       To get the pearl and gold,
       And ours to hold
Virginia
Earth's only paradise.

—From *Ode to the Virginian Voyage*, 1607
Michael Drayton, English poet (1563–1631)

The pines seem to touch the sky in this image shot by Harry C. Mann at Cape Henry, *c.* 1907. As the sun sets on the beach and 'twixt the pines, hues of red, fiery orange, and yellow lit the sky and melted slowly into the thin clouds above, casting evening shadows on the expansive beaches of "Virginia / Earth's only paradise."

IMAGES
of America

VIRGINIA BEACH
JEWEL RESORT
OF THE ATLANTIC

Amy Waters Yarsinske

ARCADIA

First published 1998
Copyright © Amy Waters Yarsinske, 1998

ISBN 0-7524-0932-8

Published by Arcadia Publishing,
an imprint of Tempus Publishing, Inc.
2 Cumberland Street, Charleston SC 29401.
Printed in Great Britain

Library of Congress Cataloging-in-Publication Data applied for

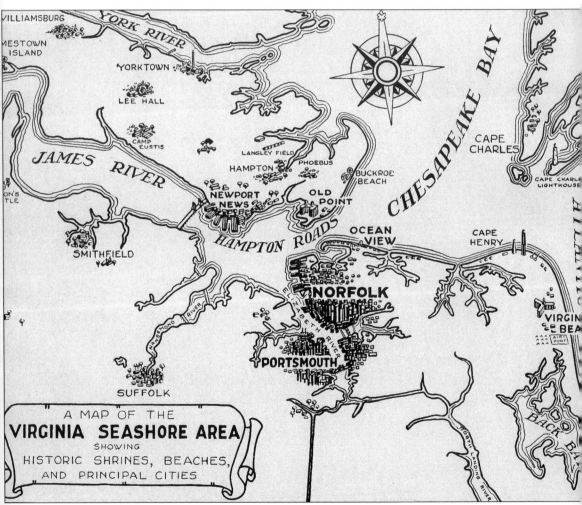

This map was drawn of Virginia's resort beaches in 1930 as a promotional for the chambers of commerce in Norfolk, Virginia Beach, Hampton, and Newport News.

Contents

Acknowledgments

I would like to extend my deepest appreciation to the many individuals and institutions who made invaluable contributions to this project. I am particularly grateful for the use of materials from the Sargeant Memorial Room, Kirn Library, and the assistance of Peggy A. Haile; Edgar T. Brown, historian and genealogist; Fielding Lewis Tyler, executive director of the Old Coast Guard Station; Carlos Wilson, director of guest services at the Cavalier Hotel; Dr. Peter B. Schultz, professor and director, Hampton Roads Agricultural Research and Extension Center; and the innumerable Virginia Beach natives and residents who contributed information and photographs for the book. Though several of the Charles S. Borjes and Jim Mays photographs originated with the Sargeant Memorial Room, others did not. The pleasure of authoring this book was the diversity of photograph and artwork resources with which I had to work. In particular instances, the resource is noted under the photograph or artwork. The Old Coast Guard Station on the oceanfront is one of the jewels in Virginia Beach's crown and its staff, in a word, superb. Fielding Tyler and Ann C. Dearman, the station's education and program director, run an outstanding museum and resource center.

As always, this book is dedicated to my husband, Raymond, and our children, Ashley, Allyson, and Raymond III. Without their love, encouragement, and unwavering patience, none of my books would be possible.

Harry C. Mann took this photograph of the waves of the Atlantic lapping the shores of Virginia Beach, c. 1907. Mann spent weeks at a time documenting the natural beauty of Cape Henry and Virginia Beach, and in this particular picture, the vastness of the sea. The marriage of sea and shore gave birth to Virginia Beach, the jewel resort of the Atlantic.

Introduction

You have to picture in your mind's eye a resplendent, enchantingly beautiful sun, waters blue as the sky, sand hills as large as small mountains, and wide white beaches littered with sea foam—the breath of the sea—and perfect seashells that are beckoning to be discovered by occasional passersby. Tall stands of stately pine and cedar hugged the dunes and whispered softly in the gentle breeze off the ocean. The Virginia Beach of yesteryear was a panorama of unparalleled scenic beauty that took centuries to achieve.

Long ago, an unknown newspaper reporter remarked that "to most people a camera is simply a photographic instrument that makes possible the perpetuating of a face, or group, or building, or scene in black and white by chemical manipulation. To them, the taking of a picture is purely a mechanical and somewhat mysterious operation that has to be conducted first in the sunlight and then in the dark." Harry C. Mann would change that perception of photography with his images of the beaches of Virginia Beach, Cape Henry, and that portion of the Virginia Beach resort that fronts the Chesapeake Bay. The images in this work taken by Mann demonstrate the innate talent of a person who never held a camera in his hand before 1907. He photographed just about anything in which he found enjoyment and sheer beauty. Of all the photographers included in the book, his pictures of the natural beauty that once defined Virginia Beach's expansive resort and residential areas, and its untamed reaches, are the most enduring. In less than one hundred years, timeless beauty would be transformed to attraction. The jewel resort of the Atlantic would be born, birthed by man's allurement with sea and its unspoiled beaches.

Harry C. Mann captured the tranquility of the dunes on a cloudy day at Cape Henry, c. 1907.

7

Three contestants competing in the first Miss Virginia pageant pose for an unknown cameraman on the beach near Seaside Park in 1926. This was also the first beauty pageant to be held at Virginia Beach.

One

Summer Cottages and A Few Hotels

"The whispering waves were half asleep,
The clouds were gone to play,
And on the woods, and on the deep,
The smile of Heaven lay."
—From *The Pine Forest of Cascine near Pisa*, 1821,
published 1824
Percy Bysshe Shelley, English poet (1792–1822)

Virginia Beach pine forests were so close to the sea that the future beach resort garnered a reputation by 1900 as lying "twixt ocean and pines," and became as famous for its magnificent stands of trees and nature trails as its seaside pleasures. An unknown photographer took this photograph in 1896.

INVESTING IN A RESORT DESTINATION

Colonel Marshall Parks, a well-known developer and entrepreneur from Norfolk, was the first person with the vision to invest in Virginia Beach as a resort destination. He constructed a wooden pavilion at the end of Seventeenth Street in 1880, which would become the first building of the new resort. He established the Seaside Hotel and Land Company to facilitate the purchase of lots from farmers with oceanfront property. Princess Anne County's seashore property was owned at that time by numerous county natives. Between 1880 and 1882, Parks' land company bought eleven farms consisting of 1,350 acres and extending 5 miles along the Atlantic shoreline. He envisioned this deserted stretch of beach as a seaside health and pleasure resort, not a new idea by any means because it had been done with great success along the New Jersey coast. Parks did want to turn the Seatack area into an exciting resort experience. In 1882, he established the Norfolk and Virginia Beach Railroad & Improvement Company, which, in turn, assumed control of the Seaside Hotel and Land Company property along the oceanfront. A rail connection was completed to Virginia by 1883. Between July 28 and September 30, 1883, 6,565 people visited Virginia Beach to dance, picnic, and play in the surf.

In 1884, Marshall Parks' company built the Virginia Beach Hotel at Fourteenth Street and Atlantic Avenue. This three-story wood-frame structure had spacious oceanfront verandas. Within three years of the hotel's construction, the railroad and land company were sold in foreclosure and later reformed under a plan devised by Pennsylvania real estate developer Charles W. Mackey. The Virginia Beach Hotel was expanded by fifty rooms, bringing its total number to 139. In its early history, the hotel attracted the likes of Alexander Graham Bell, Cornelius Vanderbilt, labor leader Samuel Gompers, politician William Jennings Bryan, and President Benjamin Harrison. The name of the hotel was changed to the Princess Anne in 1888 under the management of Simeon E. Crittenden of Cooperstown, New York. The spacious Princess Anne Hotel took up two blocks between Fourteenth and Sixteenth Streets and was connected to the railroad at its front door. The photograph above was taken in 1896. The sun parlor is the glassed-in area to the far right. (Photographer unknown.)

This postcard of the Princess Anne Hotel and wooden boardwalk is an undivided back, meaning it was published between 1901 and 1907 at a time when the U.S. Post Office did not allow a message to be written on the reverse side. The card was produced by Raphael Tuck & Sons, renowned as "art publishers to their Majesties the King and Queen," as part of postcard series No. 2223, "Landmarks of Virginia." The view is looking south from Seventeenth Street.

Railroads would play the key role in opening up the area from Cape Henry to Virginia Beach. Cape Henry had the most beautiful land of the two. When Cape Henry was opened for private sale of its land upon approval by the Virginia General Assembly in 1866, only a few cottages were constructed. The reason was due primarily to lack of easy access. There were no rail lines to Cape Henry until the Chesapeake Transit Company traversed Lynnhaven Inlet, shown here in the photograph above, with an electric rail line from Norfolk to Cape Henry in 1902, the same year the picture was taken by an unknown photographer. The bridge had a draw to permit boats to pass. The rail bridge was closed to train traffic in 1926, when its track was planked over for Norfolk Southern Bus Company buses to transport people to Cape Henry. The Lesner Bridge was built two years later, ending the use of the crossing forever. It was torn down in 1953.

The Chesapeake Transit Company laid the first track to Cape Henry in 1902, the year the above picture was taken. The train shown here has just left the depot north of the old lighthouse. The depot, pictured below on a postcard as it appeared about the same year, was a busy point of destination as people came by the thousands to visit Cape Henry's famous beaches and sand hills. The station is still standing. The U.S. Army devised an adaptive reuse of the building and, today, it is the headquarters building for the Eleventh Transportation Battalion at Fort Story. (Postcard courtesy of Edgar T. Brown.)

Electric Railroad Depot, Cape Henry, near Norfolk, Va.

The Chesapeake Transit Company's Cape Henry train used the same broad-gauge rail line to which the Norfolk and Southern Railroad had converted in 1897. The company had its trains running from Cape Henry south to Virginia Beach by 1898, and then a rather unexpected turn of events occurred—the Norfolk and Southern Railroad started laying its own broad-gauge track north, but next to existing Chesapeake Transit Company line. Employees of the Chesapeake Transit Company tried to remove their competitor's track under cover of darkness. This was unsuccessful. Rather than enter a protracted competition to see who could thwart the other's expansion plans, the Chesapeake Transit Company bought stock in the Norfolk and Southern Railroad, and basically merged the companies' efforts. After a reorganization, the Norfolk and Southern Railway ran the electric loop from Norfolk to Cape Henry to Virginia Beach and back to downtown Norfolk. The photograph shows the Norfolk, Cape Henry & Virginia Beach line, No. 4, of the Norfolk and Southern in 1904, the year this new service began. (Photographer unknown.)

Harry C. Mann captured several important structures in his 1909 photograph of the Cape Henry lighthouses. Perhaps the most important was William J. O'Keefe's famous casino and oyster house, the large structure between the lighthouses. O'Keefe used to walk the beach from his small hotel at the corner of Sixteenth Street and Atlantic Avenue to the lighthouses. He enjoyed the landscape so much that he decided to build his legendary establishment, known as the Cape Henry Casino, on the oceanfront directly in line with the little brick train depot at Cape Henry, located just north of the old Cape Henry light. His casino was the place to go. The menu included Smithfield ham and oysters served any way the customer wanted them: raw, roasted or fried. President William Howard Taft visited O'Keefe's by rail car in November 1909.

William J. O'Keefe's establishment at Cape Henry opened on July 4, 1903. Though known as Cape Henry Casino, patrons just called it simply "O'Keefe's Casino." The roasting of oysters, taken from a postcard photographed by Harry C. Mann, c. 1910, was a valued art form to casino owner O'Keefe. On the evening of President William Howard Taft's visit to the casino in November 1909, O'Keefe offered a prize for the prettiest barrel of oysters brought to him by his oyster suppliers who plied the Lynnhaven River. In the end, there was no winner declared because O'Keefe decided they were all too beautiful to choose just one. (Courtesy of Edgar T. Brown.)

Not all of the cottages at Cape Henry were as attractive as those along the Virginia Beach shore. The Hancock family, residents of the Lafayette-Winona section of Norfolk, had a cottage that was little more than a shack on the water's edge. The picture postcard above was taken in 1906 and shows members of the Hancock family on a visit to the cottage. In the accompanying photograph of the Tidewater Pleasure Club, taken in front of the same cottage in 1896, one of the Hancock boys is standing fourth from the left in the front row. Members of the club were photographed by an unknown photographer during an oyster roast at Cape Henry. While some enjoyed raw oysters on the shell, others indulged in Lynnhaven oyster stew and, of course, liquid spirits.

Watermen brought many kinds of sea life to Hopkins Fish & Oyster Company in Norfolk's Atlantic City for processing. This loggerhead turtle, taken off Cape Henry, was one such catch. Turtle meat and soup could be found on the menus of several restaurants and hotels in Norfolk and Portsmouth. The loggerhead turtle has been listed as an endangered species since 1978, and is considered vulnerable by the International Union for the Conservation of Nature. Native to Atlantic waters, the loggerhead may reach a weight of 450 pounds, though a 250- to 300-pound animal with a 3-foot back shell is considered large. Loggerheads reach maturity between twenty and thirty years and roughly 200 pounds. The Virginia-Carolina coast is a favorite breeding and feeding ground of the loggerhead. They prefer a diet of hermit crabs, shellfish, conches, Portuguese men-of-war, sponges, jellyfish, and fish. The picture shown here was taken about 1910 by an unknown photographer.

Pine forests sprinkled with sand, swamps, and inland waterways ran up to the dune line at Virginia Beach. In the deepest recesses of the woods, dogwood and wild plum, jasmine and bayberry, poplar and field maple, oak and pine, each had its tint and season. Much of the scenery of Harry C. Mann's picture had changed little since the day Christopher Newport's expedition set foot on the sands of Cape Henry for the first time in 1607. Aside from the power line strung along the beach, this is an untouched landscape with an extraordinary view of the ocean, c. 1910.

This striped bass was harvested near Cape Henry about 1910. A worker at Hopkins Fish & Oyster Company shows off the prize catch. Striped bass are found from the Gulf of St. Lawrence to Florida. Though they were plentiful in Virginia-Carolina waters during the period in which the photograph was taken, the area from Cape Cod to Cape May is now the place where they are most plentiful. A very popular game fish, striped bass can attain a length of 5 1/2 feet and weigh as much as 125 pounds. The striped bass line record was achieved in 1913 with a fish that weighed 73 pounds and grew to 5 feet in length.

One of the first hostelries at Cape Henry was the Hygeia, Roe & Dyer, proprietors. Located at what was then Thirty-seventh Street, the establishment played host to the myriad of vacationers who visited the beautiful shores and pine forests at the north end of Virginia Beach. The postcard was photographed by Brooks & Cowling, and mailed August 26, 1909, from Cape Henry, Virginia, to Jefferson, Maryland. (Courtesy of Edgar T. Brown.)

The Princess Anne Hotel, on the left, anchored the Virginia Beach shoreline and boardwalk at the time this photograph was taken in 1902. A couple of ladies in their finery were strolling down the beach, but paused long enough to look back at the cameraman.

Virginia Beach had summer cottages and a few hotels in the early years of the twentieth century. Known as the Cottage Line, these privately and commercially-owned cottages lent character and distinction to the oceanfront. This Harry C. Mann photograph, taken c. 1910, shows the wooden boardwalk constructed in 1888. The Arlington Hotel, its flag flying in front, was located just south of Thirteenth Street. The Arlington was an early hotel at the beach and an important one after the Princess Anne Hotel burned to the ground on June 10, 1907. The Baptist Church of Virginia bought the Arlington in the 1910s for its summer retreats. Part of the Atkinson Cottage is visible to the extreme left of the picture. The cottage in full-view, left foreground, is the Burton Cottage. From Burton Cottage on down the Cottage Line stood the Carrington Cottage, also known as the Mount Vernon, and the DeWitt Cottage. The windmill on the left pumped water for the Holland home and some of the other cottages. Beyond the DeWitt Cottage was the Glennan Cottage, Arlington Hotel, Booth Cottage, Ferebee Cottage, and the Raleigh Bar. Only the DeWitt Cottage stands today.

THE FLUME

The Flume is the large wooden trough at Thirteenth Street in the upper right of this photograph of the Cottage Line. The Flume was conceived by Bernard P. Holland, the first mayor, postmaster, and telegrapher of the town of Virginia Beach. It was intended to aid in the eradication of mosquitoes. The device carried saltwater from the Atlantic Ocean two blocks inland to Lake Holly, considered prime breeding ground for the king of summer pests—the mosquito. Holland figured the regular infusion of saltwater into a freshwater lake would make the lake highly undesirable for mosquitoes. His plan worked, but on the down side, it had a negative environmental impact on the lake's natural fish and wildlife, a diverse assortment of critters who turned their noses at saltwater. The Flume made an ideal fishing pier for the locals, and children could place small rowboats at the landed-end of Atlantic Avenue and the wave action sent them on a delightful joy ride into Lake Holly. Children had incredible fun doing this until caught by their parents, who considered the adventure a bit unsafe.

Casino at Cape Henry, Va.

O'Keefe's Casino was as popular as ever when this postcard was sent on January 20, 1913. The casino had seen the likes of President Taft, Andrew Carnegie, and numerous notables in its heyday. The image on the postcard was taken by Harry C. Mann, one of Hampton Roads' most famous photographers from 1906 to 1922. (Courtesy of Edgar T. Brown.)

View of Boardwalk, Virginia Beach Summer Resort, near Norfolk, Va.

Harry C. Mann turned one of his finest photographs of the first boardwalk into a postcard. The sender of the postcard, dated August 19, 1911, said, "We like this place very much. Are in a lovely large cottage. It's lovely and cool and the ocean was simply grand last night so rough." Beach patrons could purchase ice cream, soda water, candy, souvenirs, and postcards in the establishment shown in the lower right corner of the card. Mann was standing just above Fourteenth Street looking south. From the composition of the photographic image used on the card, it could not have been taken prior to 1908. The Raleigh Bar was established after the Princess Anne Hotel burned in 1907, and the owners of the bar had salvaged the bar from the saloon of the hotel. (Courtesy of Edgar T. Brown.)

This is an interior view of the Knights Templar Club, c. 1915. The Knights Templars, a secret society, had their own building on Third Street, off Shore Drive, until June 1927, when C.M. Emerson and A.A. Vaughan formed a corporation known as the Hygeia Club and assumed ownership of the old structure. At various times the club changed hands and names. By 1936, it was a dance hall called Club 500, and it became a popular spot for big bands to play. In the late 1940s, the property was sold to the Virginia Beach Shriners and renamed the Templar Club once again. The site of the Knights Templar Club is now occupied by the McDonald's restaurant and Seagate Colony condominiums at the foot of Old Great Neck Road and Shore Drive. (Photographer unknown.)

The Chalfonte Hotel, located at Twenty-eighth Street and the oceanfront, was photographed c. 1925. The hotel proffered superb dining and dancing and became an immediate attraction for young people from Norfolk. The Chalfonte was near Seaside Park. A narrow sidewalk coupled with the broad stretch of sand in the foreground indicates that this photograph pre-dates the construction of the concrete promenade begun in 1926, but not opened to the public until 1927.

The Courtney Terrace at Virginia Beach was photographed by an unknown photographer on May 3, 1928. Courtney Terrace was located at Sixteenth Street and the oceanfront, but began in 1902 as a little hostelry called O'Keefe's Inn. William J. O'Keefe constructed his original inn on the southeast corner of Sixteenth Street and Atlantic Avenue. As the beach resort grew, O'Keefe decided to jack up the inn and move it across the street to the oceanfront where he renamed it Courtney Terrace. After several additions, the hotel seen in this photograph was complete. The concrete promenade, shown here, was completed in 1927. The Courtney Terrace was demolished in 1959.

An artist's conception of the Ocean Plaza Hotel, rendered in 1925, depicts another project that was purportedly to join the Virginia Beach resort strip. Within the decade of the 1920s, many of the resort's most attractive hostelries would be built, but not this one. The project never came to fruition. The structure's expensive Spanish, specifically Moorish-style, architecture would have been similar to Ocean View's Nansemond Hotel.

The Traymore Apartments (lower right) and the Pinewood Hotel (left of the Traymore) were two of a long succession of successful Virginia Beach developments by Jacob Laskin and his sons, Elmer and Louis. The Laskins were prosperous resort real estate investors from Mount Vernon, New York. They had already done well for themselves in the Florida market and saw Virginia Beach's oceanfront as another opportunity to extend their real estate holdings on the Atlantic coast. By 1926, the Laskins were well on their way to completion of a series of highly profitable Virginia Beach projects, including the Pinewood Hotel and Traymore Apartments, shown here *c.* 1930. The Pinewood was attractive to visitors not only for its oceanfront access, but the number of activities provided by the hotel, including badminton, tennis, and handball. What remains of the Pinewood is part of the Dunes Motor Inn at Tenth Street and the oceanfront. The Traymore Apartments were apartments until 1946, but the building itself was razed in 1983. Barclay Towers was constructed on the site. The Laskins have one quite prominent reminder of their legacy to Virginia Beach—Laskin Road. The road from Virginia Beach Boulevard to Thirty-first Street was completed in 1926. (Photographer unknown.)

Two

Sea Breezes and Incomparable Landscapes

"To the ocean now I fly,
And those happy climes that lie
Where day never shuts his eye,
Up in the broad fields of the sky."
—From "The Spirit Epiloguizes," *Comus*
John Milton, English poet (1608–1674)

Harry C. Mann captured the beauty of the Cape Henry beaches in this *c.* 1907 photograph. "I saw the daughters of the ocean dance / With wind and tide, and heard them on the rocks; / White hands they waved me, tossing sunlit locks, / Green as the light an emerald holds in trance" [Unknown French poet].

Harry C. Mann took this c. 1907 photograph of the Cape Henry desert. "The gray sea and the long black land; / And the yellow half-moon large and low; / And the startled little waves that leap / In fiery ringlets from their sleep" [from *Meeting at Night*; Robert Browning, English poet (1812–1889)].

EXPLORATION AND DISCOVERY

The coastline from Virginia Beach to Cape Henry is geographically a continuation of the barrier reef that forms the coast of the Carolinas. This barrier reef protects the harbor of Hampton Roads. Spanish explorers mapped the Cape Henry coast in the sixteenth century, and it is these ill-fated travelers who left so many shipwrecks along the Virginia Beach coast. There was a Spanish expedition in 1570 to the Virginia Capes. They mapped Crystal Lake, where Spanish ships are known to have anchored. Moving into the Chesapeake Bay, the same expedition encountered the Ajacàn tribe. The Ajacàns turned on the Spaniards, killing five priests and four novices of the Society of Jesus who had tried to convert them to Christianity. The Englishmen who arrived in 1607 were greatly impressed by the natural beauty of Cape Henry. They observed "flowers of divers kinds and colors and goodly trees," but they encountered warriors of the Chesapeake tribe who attacked the Englishmen under cover of darkness. Captain George Percy described two of their party being wounded, one by the name of Matthew Morton, seriously. Percy recorded, "We came to a place where they had made a great fire, and had been newly roasting oysters. When they perceived our coming, they fled away to the mountains, and left many of the oysters in the fire. We ate some of the oysters, which were very large and delicate in taste." The mountains to which Percy refers were the Antaean tree-covered sand dunes that rose nearly a hundred feet high at Cape Henry. The oysters were, of course, the famous Lynnhaven oysters.

The dunes at Cape Henry lay softly, brushed ever-so-gently by a cool summer breeze at sunset, *c.* 1907. (Harry C. Mann, photographer.)

HARRY C. MANN AND THE MAGIC OF THE SEA

Harry C. Mann brought photography to its highest point of development, to an art form we can admire and respect even today. He knew little to nothing about taking pictures prior to 1907, but he had the good fortune of having a brother, Colonel James Mann, who was a counsel for the Jamestown Photographic Corporation, the group responsible for taking official photographs of the exposition grounds, activities, and dignitaries. He was given a position with the corporation, at which time he was lured by association to staff photographers and cameras to the picture-taking profession. He started with pictures of rather mundane scenes to learn the trade. The first photographic equipment he ever owned was a small, four-by-five camera that he used to snap wooded vistas and beach scenes. Mann later owned a couple of eight-by-ten and five-by-seven plate cameras. He loved the endless rapture of the sea, sky, and dunes at Cape Henry in Virginia Beach. His photographs evoke fond memories of untouched sand dunes and gorgeous sunsets, or the power of a storm rising over the water. With practice, Mann became one of the foremost artist photographers in the United States—his pictures winning accolades from London and Paris to New York. He was published in *National Geographic* as well as numerous newspapers nationwide. For a time, he maintained a studio at the corner of Main and Bank Streets in downtown Norfolk. Born in Petersburg, Virginia, on June 8, 1866, Mann died at the age of sixty on December 12, 1926, in Lynchburg, Virginia.

A four-masted top-sail schooner anchored in Lynnhaven Bay, c. 1907, and was caught in this beautiful setting by photographer Harry C. Mann. "The harbor-bay was clear as glass, / So smoothly was it strewn! / And on the bay the moonlight lay / And the shadow of the moon, / And the bay was white with silent light" [From *The Rime of the Ancient Mariner*, 1798; Samuel Taylor Coleridge, English poet (1772–1834)].

Linkhorn Bay sparkled as the setting sun peeked through cloudy skies and backlit the trees in the foreground, *c.* 1907. (Harry C. Mann, photographer.)

The twisted remnants of trees stood atop Sand Hill at Cape Henry, *c.* 1907. "We paused amid the pine that stood / The giants of the waste, / Tortured by storms to shapes as rude / With stems like serpents interlaced" [From *The Pine Forest of the Cascine Near Pisa*, 1821, published 1824; Percy Bysshe Shelley, English poet (1792–1822)].

"A dream of silence and of peace." The wooded reaches of Linkhorn Bay presented a compelling picture for photographer Harry C. Mann, c. 1907. Mann was clearly entranced by

the flickering image of clouds dancing across the still water and the shadows of pine, which brought tranquility to his final photograph.

There are no written records to document the history of Cape Henry's most notorious historic figures. Pirates and wreckers used the sand wastes as headquarters for their illegal activities. Tales of Blackbeard and his treasure abound. Along the edge of Long Creek, located between Lynnhaven and Broad Bay, there is a hill much higher than any other dune that stood at Cape Henry. It was called Blackbeard's Hill. Harry C. Mann spent weeks at a time photographing Cape Henry between 1907 and 1910. This image, taken c. 1907, is purportedly of Blackbeard's Hill. Legend also has it that men would mark the entrance points to the Cape with beacon fires. Wreckers would spot the fires and capture the beacon crew, then move the fire to the south. This would pull the ships aground at Cape Henry where wreckers waited to take their cargo and, more often than not, kill the ship's crew.

Harry C. Mann had many of his Cape Henry and Virginia Beach photographs manufactured as postcards, though a significant number of his designs were subsequently altered and sold by unscrupulous manufacturers. The easiest method of telling a real Mann postcard from the impersonator is in the photograph. Once a Mann photograph and its postcard are held side-by-side, the original work becomes easy to spot. This image of Sand Hill at Cape Henry, *c.* 1907, is a Mann. It shows visitors climbing the mountain-size dune. Sand Hill marked the transition point between the Chesapeake Bay and Atlantic Ocean. Continuously shifting in size and dimension and always growing larger, it is thought to have taken centuries for this mountain of sand to accumulate to the height seen in Mann's postcard.

Water lilies in Lake Bradford presented a picturesque scene for photographer Harry C. Mann, *c.* 1907.

"Now came still evening on, and twilight grey / Hath in her sober livery all things clad" [From "Evening in Paradise," *Paradise Lost*; John Milton, English poet (1608–1674)].

"But such a tide as moving seems asleep, / Too full for sound and foam, / When that which drew from out the boundless deep / Turns again home" [From *Crossing the Bar*; Alfred, Lord Tennyson (1809–1892)].

"The wind is harrowing the dunes tonight, / It mocks the sea and hisses at the moon, / Bends slender trees, and like a lyric sprite / Plays on the broken reeds a plaintive tune, / And twirls the sand in spirals thin and white . . ." [From *Wind on the Dunes*; John Richard Moreland, American poet (n.d.)]. The moving dunes at Cape Henry aptly fit the words of philosopher Horace, who wrote, "a picture is a poem without words." When Harry C. Mann photographed the shifting sands of Virginia Beach, *c.* 1907, he created images for which there are few words to adequately express their beauty and immortality.

"In the skirts of the thunder cloud; now down the sweep / Of the wind-cloven wave to the chasm of the deep" (From *A Vision of the Sea*, 1820; Percy Bysshe Shelley, English poet (1792–1822)].

"Round the cape of a sudden came the sea, / And the sun looked over the mountain's rim" [From *Parting at Morning*; Robert Browning, English poet (1812–1889)].

Perhaps one of the most beautiful series of photographs Harry C. Mann ever took of Cape Henry and Virginia Beach were the winter scenes. Here, the snow envelopes the dunes like a soft white blanket mingling gently with the shifting sands. The picture was taken *c.* 1907 and is a reminder of the beauty of the changing seasons on the beach.

"A wind's in the heart of me, a fire's in my heels, / I am tired of brick and stone and rumbling wagon-wheels; / I hunger for the sea's edge, the limits of the land, / Where the wild old Atlantic is shouting on the sand" [From A *Wanderer's Song*, 1902; John Masefield, English poet laureate (1878–1967)]. As the sands kiss the shore at Cape Henry, *c.* 1907, the journey's just begun. (Harry C. Mann, photographer.)

Virginia Beach was famous for its pine forests as much as its resplendent beaches. Harry C. Mann photographed both places extensively between 1907 and 1910. "We wandered to the Pine Forest / That skirts the Ocean's foam, / The lightest wind was in its nest, / The tempest in its home" [(From *The Pine Forest of the Cascine near Pisa*, 1821, published 1824; Percy Bysshe Shelley, English poet (1792–1822)].

"Only, from the long line of spray / Where the sea meets the moon-blanched land, / Listen! you hear the grating roar / Of pebbles which the waves draw back" [From *Dover Beach*; Matthew Arnold, English poet (1822–1888)].

A first line battleship of the U.S. Navy, USS *Utah* (BB-31), steams past Cape Henry behind a five-masted top-sail schooner loaded with cargo and riding low in the water. The year was 1911. The *Utah*, like each of the first line battleships of her era, can be identified by her unique hull, superstructure, and armament features. The keel of the *Utah* was laid by New York Shipbuilding Company of Camden, New York, on March 15, 1909. The *Utah* was commissioned into service on August 31, 1911. She operated off four Parsons Turbine engines powered by twelve boilers. Her main battery included 10- to 12-inch forty-five caliber guns in five turrets; the secondary battery had sixteen 5-inch fifty-one caliber guns, eight 3-inch fifty caliber antiaircraft guns, four 3-pounder saluting guns, and two 21-inch torpedo tubes. The *Utah* carried 64 officers and 1,260 enlisted men. (Harry C. Mann, photographer.)

Harry C. Mann photographed three first line battleships of the U.S. Navy steaming south off Cape Henry on patrol in 1912. The ships are (from left to right) the USS *Utah*, USS *Delaware* (BB-28), and USS *Florida* (BB-30). The USS *Delaware* was the oldest of the three. She was built by Newport News Shipbuilding and Drydock Company and commissioned in 1910. The *Delaware*'s crew complement was 64 officers and 1,262 enlisted men. As a result of the Disarmament Treaty of Navies, signed October 1, 1923, the *Delaware* was sold in 1924. The USS *Florida* was constructed at the Navy Yard in New York and commissioned on September 15, 1911. Identification was possible through time frame of use, placement and construction of superstructure—the "wire cage" visible on each ship—and hull and armament configuration as well as the service record of each battleship. The Navy utilized the double cage with double stacks on a distinct grouping of its battleships before going to double cage with one stack and making numerous alterations to the battleships' superstructure and hull designs.

"O the beach at night alone, / As the old mother sways her to and fro singing her husky song, / As I watch the bright stars shining, I think a thought of the clef / of the universes and of the future" [From *On the Beach at Night*, 1856; Walt Whitman, American poet (1819–1892)]. Harry C. Mann captured the timeless beauty of the Cape Henry Desert at sunset, *c.* 1907, and thus preserved the beauty that once was and will and never be again.

This portrait of Lynnhaven Inlet was taken in 1907. The tranquility of sunset on the water conjures another Whitman line, from *The Sleepers* (1855, 1881), in which the great American poet penned, "The universe is duly in order, every thing is in its place." There are constants of the landscape that are eternal and more beautiful than words can describe. (Harry C. Mann, photographer.)

Elbert Hubbard, an experienced mariner and observer of the sea who perished on the ocean
near the turn of the century, wrote the following passage: "The sea knows all things for at night
when the winds are asleep the stars confide to him their secrets . . . in its depths they have seen
mirrored the image of Eternity—of Infinity . . ." Harry C. Mann captured Hubbard's words in
the rapture of his moment with the sea, c. 1907.

Three

The Wild Country of Back Bay and Croatan

"Only the soul that goes,
Eager. Eager. Flying.
Over the globe of the moon,
Over the wood that glows.
Wings linked. Necks a-strain,
A rush and a wild crying."
—From *The Wild Duck*
John Masefield, English poet laureate
(1878–1967)

Back Bay actually consists of five separate bays: North Bay, Shipps Bay, Redhead Bay, Sand Bay, and Back Bay. There are 63,000 acres of water and marsh in this area of what is now the city of Virginia Beach. During the late nineteenth century, bass and white perch were the bulwark of a healthy fishing industry, but as the early years of the twentieth century slipped by, fishing tapered off. Back Bay is on the Atlantic flyway for migratory birds. Market gunners were permitted in the bay to hunt birds for commercial customers such as hotels, restaurants, and markets until 1925 when they were outlawed from the back bays. At one time, canvasbacks and redheads were the most plentiful wildfowl in Back Bay, but their populations had diminished significantly by the 1930s. The Canadian geese in this photograph were indicative of the plenitude of their species, and game birds in general, which once sought refuge in Back Bay. Charles S. Borjes took the picture on October 1, 1925.

Market gunners had gone to the reaches of Back Bay and returned with plenty of wildfowl for the restaurants and hotels in downtown Norfolk, *c.* 1900. (Photographer unknown.)

The Drum Point Hunting Club was a gunning club in Back Bay. Charles S. Borjes photographed the clubhouse on October 1, 1925.

The Ragged Island Gunning Club (pictured here, October 1, 1925) was the home of the Ragged Island Gunning Association of Virginia, a group that enjoyed a national reputation for its activities and noteworthy membership. Located in the center of Virginia Beach's marshes and waters teeming with wild celery and other choice foods for waterfowl were the Ragged Islands—the origin of the club's name and location of its building. Records from the old Princess Anne Courthouse revealed that in 1737 His Majesty King George II, by letters of patent, graciously granted to "Sir William Gooch, Esq., Lieutenant Governor of His Majesty's Ancient and Great Colony and Dominion of Virginia, and Commander-in-Chief of the forces at Williamsburg; certain islands in Back Bay, Princess Anne County, known as 'Ragged Islands.' " The grantee and later his descendants held the title to these rich game lands until about 1880, and the game land was freely hunted over by the residents of that section. In 1880, the property passed through the Court of Chancery into the hands of a number of gentlemen who formed under the Ragged Island Gunning Club. Acquisition of the title was followed by the erection of a well-equipped clubhouse that was destined to entertain many famous men. The Ragged Island Gunning Club was torn down and its land incorporated as part of the Back Bay National Wildlife Refuge. (Charles S. Borjes, photographer.)

The Croatan Club, pictured c. 1930, derived its name from the word "CROATAN," carved on a tree by a member of the Lost Colony, an English colony established in the New World in 1587. The expedition, which left Plymouth, England, was led by John White and carried 120 men, women, and children to Roanoke Island on the Outer Banks of North Carolina to establish a British settlement. White returned to England for provisions in 1587, and left the colony on Roanoke Island. Three years and one month later, he returned to find everyone had disappeared, and the only communication left behind seemed to be the carving on the tree. Since there was no cross carved alongside the word—a cross indicating distress or peril—White presumed the colonists might have moved to Croatan Island. White wanted to check Croatan Island for the colonists, including the first English child born in the New World and his first grandchild, Virginia Dare, but a violent storm was fast approaching and Captain Abraham Cocke decided to depart for the West Indies rather than face almost certain destruction on the sea. Croatan Island derived its name from the Croatan tribe which inhabited the land.

The interior of the Croatan Club, a private hunting and fishing club south of Rudee Inlet at Virginia Beach, was photographed in the fall, c. 1928. Telling a tall-fish-tale—always "The fish was really that big . . ."—seems to be quite entertaining for this fisherman's compatriots. (Photographer unknown.)

Duck hunting and fresh and saltwater fishing were popular pastimes in Back Bay and the lakes near Cape Henry. These areas, in addition to the North Carolina marshes, were hunted and controlled by the Ragged Island Gunning Club and Back Bay Club. This famous ducking area was often visited by President Grover Cleveland, who often stayed at the Back Bay Club. President Benjamin Harrison hunted in the reaches of Back Bay, too. Duck blinds permeated Back Bay and the North Carolina marshes and sounds. Recreational and market gunners would access the blinds by boats such as the ones shown here on Back Bay, October 1, 1925. The quiet recesses of the five bays of Back Bay and inland waters near Cape Henry became a famous retreat for hunters of small game—even the Cape Henry Desert and its bordering tract of woodland provided excellent game for hunters. (Charles S. Borjes, photographer.)

The sport of sports in Virginia was at one time heralded by the winding horns, the deep, musical baying of hounds, and the thunder of hoofs sounding across the rolling lowlands of old Lynnhaven on a fox hunt. In this image, taken by an unknown photographer c. 1929, the hunt for the slippery fox was on. Stories of the fox and hound days of Princess Anne County are many, but one, in particular, is a classic. A story passed down through the years told that the Reverend Anthony Walke, rector of Old Donation Episcopal Church, could be ministering the Word of Life, but the minute he heard the sound of horns and cry of the hounds during any part of the service, he came down from the Chancel, mounted his horse tied in the churchyard, and off to the fox hunt he went. Walke, it is of interest to note, represented Princess Anne County at the 1788 convention at which Virginia ratified the United States Constitution.

Four
Seaman's Salvation

"I must go down to the seas again,
to the lonely sea and the sky,
And all I ask is a tall ship and a star to steer her by."
—From *Sea Fever*
John Masefield, English poet laureate
(1878–1967)

The Seatack Life Saving Station at Virginia Beach derived its placename from "Sea Attack" or the bombardment from British warships suffered by that stretch of oceanfront in the War of 1812. The station was built in 1878 on land that is now at the corner of Twenty-fourth Street and Atlantic Avenue. This photograph, taken by an unknown photographer, shows Seatack as it appeared in 1896. Notice the station's six surfmen and the keeper-in-charge in the surfboat to the right. These men, all residents of the area around Seatack, manned the station from December 1 to April 30 of the year. Seatack was part of Life Saving District Six, an area spanning Cape Henry, Virginia, to Cape Fear, North Carolina. There were five life saving stations along the Virginia Beach coastline spaced exactly 6 miles apart: Cape Henry, Dam Neck Mills, False Cape, Little Island, and Seatack. These stations, operated under the Department of Commerce, were the salvation of countless seamen in peril on the sea from 1874 to 1915, when the U.S. Coast Guard was established and assumed their duties.

Without delay, on August 9, 1790, the Commonwealth of Virginia ceded 2 acres of land at Cape Henry to the federal government upon condition that a lighthouse be erected on the site. In March 1791, the federal government concluded its contract with John McComb Jr., bricklayer, to build and equip a lighthouse at a cost of $17,500. He completed the stone structure, the first one ever constructed by the federal government, that year. McComb, it should be noted, was a master architect of the post-colonial style. He designed the Old City Hall in New York City. Benjamin Henry Latrobe (1764–1820), undoubtedly the most renowned architect and engineer of his time, observed after a visit to Cape Henry in 1798, "it was placed upon the highest hill at the Cape. It is a good solid building of Rappahannock free-stone." The lighthouse is octagonal in shape. The Harry C. Mann photograph of the old Cape Henry lighthouse was taken c. 1907.

LEGISLATING A LIGHTHOUSE

Petitions to erect a lighthouse at Cape Henry appeared for the first time in the Henning Statutes, page thirty-five, Volume II, dated March 23, 1660. An increase in trade passing between the Virginia Capes, Cape Henry and Cape Charles, necessitated the call for beacons to guide seafarers to safe port. A lighthouse was not built on the basis of this petition. On November 24, 1720, the governor of Virginia sent a message to the General Assembly. The Journal of the House of Burgesses, page 288, dated Friday, December 2, resolved, "That a Light House at Cape Henry will be useful and of great advantage to all ships that shall come within the Capes of Virginia." The text of the full resolution was transmitted to the governor so he could contact the governor of Maryland with the proposal to build identical beacons on either side of the Capes. Nothing came of it. Lieutenant Governor William Gooch took up the cause in 1727. Gooch's bill to erect a lighthouse was read for the first time in the Assembly on March 19, 1727, and passed March 27, 1728. The difference between the two dates was not one year. The year changed from 1727 to 1728, even though only eight days had actually passed. In this period, March 25 was the first day of the legal year. About 700 B.C., Numa Pompilius, Rome's second emperor, reorganized the calendar and made March 25, the vernal equinox, the first day of the year. Despite several changes by Julius Caesar and his successors, the year's beginning remained unchanged until 1752, and then for the first time in the Virginia colony, January 1, 1752, was New Year's Day. The process of petitioning, passing resolutions, and tabling the lighthouse issue in the Assembly continued until 1789.

The Toilers of the Sea

"The Toilers of the Sea" referred to the men of the five life saving stations along the Virginia Beach coastline. These men possessed a bravery and heroism unparalleled in local history because they fought the sea for human lives. The postcard, c. 1900, was printed in Germany by K.V.G.G. Lange B.L. Schwalbach, Atlantic Coast Series No. 404. (Courtesy of Edgar T. Brown.)

SELECTION OF CAPE HENRY

In the first session of the first Congress of the United States, a law was enacted, Act 9, for "Establishment and Support of Light Houses, Beacons, Buoys and Public Piers." Only one specific site is mentioned in the act: "That a light-house shall be erected near the entrance to the Chesapeake Bay at such place, where ceded to the United States in manner aforesaid, as the President of the United States shall direct." Signers of the act were Frederick Augustus Muhlenberg, Speaker of the House; and John Adams, president of the Senate. The act was approved on August 7, 1789, by George Washington, president of the United States.

This postcard depicts a dangerous moment in a harbor pilot's profession as he climbed aboard a vessel just entering the Chesapeake Bay near Cape Henry, Virginia, c. 1905, under deteriorating weather conditions. There have been pilots of the Virginia Capes since the early 1800s. Captain Samuel Williams Wood was the founder of the Virginia Pilots Association. He was born in Hampton, Virginia, in 1806 and died there on September 11, 1874, at the age of sixty-eight. William J. O'Keefe, owner of the Cape Henry Casino, better known as O'Keefe's Casino, published the postcard, as well as many others, in an effort to bring the sea and shore to life for visitors to and residents of "the Roads." (Courtesy of Edgar T. Brown.)

The Cape Henry Life Saving Station No. 1 was located at Cape Henry in full-view of the old and new Cape Henry Lighthouses. The U.S. Congress authorized the United States Life Saving Service in 1878, though stations such as Cape Henry were already in operation. The first life saving station at Cape Henry was constructed in 1874, and the second, pictured here, in 1903. There were 185 shipwrecks off the Virginia coast between 1874 and 1915, and most of these could be attributed to radical changes in the weather which caused ships to run aground. (Courtesy of Edgar T. Brown.)

In 1879, Congress approved a contract to build a new iron lighthouse consisting of cast-iron plates backed by masonry walls. The new Cape Henry light was finished in December 1881. The railroad tracks at Cape Henry are visible behind the new light. This photograph postcard was printed by the Souvenir Post Card Company of New York, Series No. 3611, c. 1905. When actual photographs appear on a postcard, they are printed on photographic paper and have the word "Post Card" and a stamp box printed on the back. As a collectible, these postcards are the most desirable.

KEEPERS OF THE OLD LIGHT

The first lighthouse keeper was Laban Goffigan, and it is he who is thought to have lighted the tower for the first time in October 1792, using sperm oil in a common lamp, probably an Iron Lanthorne. After 1812, keepers used an Argand lamp with metallic reflectors. In 1855, a fog bell, called a Jones bell, was installed. During 1857, after constructing a brick lining in the tower from top to bottom, a dioptric Fresnel lens was installed. The Fresnel device could be seen for 24 miles, and it remained in use in the tower until it was abandoned in 1881. Captain John H. Drew of Norfolk, assistant keeper from 1862 to 1863, revisited the old light in June 1934, seventy-one years after he had left his post. He climbed the tower and surveyed the shifting sands and sea. From his recollections, much was learned of the Civil War period in the lighthouse's history. He said keepers used whale oil in his day, the supply being stored in copper tanks near the recesses in the base just inside the door. The lamp had three concentric wicks, fed by a clock-driven pump. During the Civil War, Drew recalled that in April 1861, men from Princess Anne County broke the glass around the light and sabotaged the lamps. As a result, a lightship was placed between the Capes. In Drew's day, the top of the lighthouse hill was covered by a platform of cemented stone and brick about 4 feet below the door sill. The platform was dismantled and the top of the hill lowered between 6 to 8 feet by the winds, exposing much of the foundations. The stones lying around the hill in the photograph by Mann (on page 50) had been part of the platform.

53

By far the most tragic shipwreck off Virginia Beach was the Norwegian bark *Dictator*. Memories of the *Dictator* will always remain a heartfelt, revered piece of Virginia Beach's history. This photograph, taken after the turn of the century, had an interesting inscription on the back. The message stated, in part, as follows: "After many years—and much writing—and the fact that Mr. Jorgensen come [*sic*] each year and threw a wreath of flowers, sometimes a small bunch, but he come [*sic*] regularly. Interest grew until the Municipal League, headed by Mrs. Robert W. Dail, decided to put it up in concrete." (Courtesy of Edgar T. Brown.)

THE DICTATOR AND THE NORWEGIAN LADY

The Norwegian bark *Dictator* was bound from Pensacola, Florida, to West Bartlepool, England, with a full load of timber when she encountered a couple of storms at sea that caused damage to the ship. Captain Jorgen Martinius Jorgensen, master of the bark, made the decision to head north along the Atlantic Coast and bring the *Dictator* into Norfolk for repairs, but the weather deteriorated as he reached the Virginia Capes and his ship was clearly in trouble. The date was March 27, 1891. The *Dictator* proceeded past the Princess Anne Hotel at Sixteenth Street, grounding north of the hotel in the vicinity of Fortieth Street. Surfmen from the Cape Henry and Seatack Life Saving Stations tried desperately to retrieve *Dictator*'s crewmen with a breeches buoy, but the device became entangled in the ship's rigging and was abandoned. Two *Dictator* crewmen had been saved with the breeches buoy; other crewmen that had reached a small boat were dumped into the sea and had to be rescued by surfmen. Near nightfall, the ship continued to break apart, and Captain Jorgensen, his wife, Johanne Pauline, and baby son, Carl Zealand, and several crewmen were still aboard. Though Jorgensen had tried repeatedly to get his wife to take their son and leave the ship in a small boat, she steadfastly refused. She would not leave without her husband though he assured his wife he could make it to shore in the storm, even if he had to swim. When she rebuffed his final appeal, Jorgensen strapped his son to his back, handed Johanne Pauline a life preserver, and tried to use one of the ship's ladders for buoyancy. Jorgensen lost his hold on the ladder and fell into the sea. As he fell, baby Carl was wrenched from his back by a wave and drowned. Johanne Pauline and a crewman, Jean Baptiste, were swept off the deck and drowned as well. Only nine of the seventeen crewmen of the *Dictator* survived. Jorgensen washed ashore unconscious and had to be resuscitated by life savers. The bodies of those who perished washed ashore over the next few days, including the remains of Johanne Pauline and baby Carl. They were buried at Elmwood Cemetery in Norfolk.

As a fitting tribute to the memory of those lost on the *Dictator*, the congregation of St. Luke's Episcopal Church, located on the corner of Granby and Bute Streets in Norfolk, used antique oak from the wreck of the ship for interior and exterior construction of the church. The interior doors, wainscoting, reredos, pews, and chancel furniture were crafted of light antique oak. The doors to the main entrance were antique oak covered by iron scrollwork. Construction of the church was completed on October 18, 1892. The congregation felt using the wood in a holy place was the finest way to spiritually perpetuate the lives of those so tragically lost at sea. The end result was magnificent. The life of the church, photographed by an unknown photographer in 1896, and the ship, the wreckage of which was depicted on a postcard in 1907, were short. The church was struck by lightning on May 23, 1921, and burned to the ground. (Postcard courtesy of Edgar T. Brown.)

The figurehead of the *Dictator*, known as the Norwegian Lady, washed ashore at the Princess Anne Hotel and was found by Emily Gregory, a guest at the hostelry. She married Bernard P. Holland, the first mayor of the town of Virginia Beach. For several seasons, the Norwegian Lady faced south as she sat in front of the hotel at Sixteenth Street. In later years, she was mounted in concrete and turned to face the sea. Three little ladies posed with the figurehead on April 19, 1895, four years after the Norwegian Lady was found by Emily Gregory. (Courtesy of the Old Coast Guard Station.)

The area around the base of the Cape Henry lighthouses had grown remarkably when this postcard appeared about 1910. The three-story building to the left of the new light was the Cape Henry Weather Station, originally established on December 15, 1873, in a one-story building closer to the old light. In 1878, the weather station moved to the building shown here, then a two-story structure that had a third-floor addition made shortly after the turn of the century. The houses that appear around the new light were residences for the keepers and weather station personnel. The large antenna between the lighthouses provided telegraph transmissions for the weather service.

Old Donation Episcopal Church, located on North Witchduck Road, was the third Lynnhaven Parish edifice, accepted into vestry on June 25, 1736. The name "Old Donation" originated in 1776, when Reverend Robert Dickson willed the land adjoining his property to the parish. A free school was endowed for poor boys of the church. After the Revolutionary War, Americans cast aside anything reminding them of England, including their Anglican religious heritage, and as a result, the church property was abandoned and allowed to deteriorate. The establishment of the Protestant Episcopal Church of Virginia in 1785 might have spelled new life for Old Donation, but Reverend John G. Hull, rector of the state organization, opted to reorganize the parish in 1842, and built a new structure known as Emmanuel Episcopal Church. Old Donation was abandoned completely. The church sat empty for forty years and in 1882, was gutted by a forest fire that swept the north end of Witchduck. In order to prevent the church's land from reverting to the Commonwealth of Virginia's ownership, a religious service had to be held at least once each year on site. Thurmer Hoggard IV took up the cause to save Old Donation from state hands, and it was he who organized and led loyal parishioners to annual pilgrimages in the church ruins. This first picture of Old Donation was shot by Harry C. Mann during one of the pilgrimages, *c.* 1910. The image of these faithful parishioners is incredibly beautiful, Mann's composition superb. About 1912, formal plans were made to raise money to rebuild the church to its former splendor and in 1916, Old Donation's restoration was complete.

This image of Old Donation was taken on Tuesday, October 20, 1908, by an unknown photographer.

Pilot Boat Relief.   Cape Henry, Va.

Hand-colored postcards such as this one were considered of high quality. The scene was intended to show pilot boat relief near Cape Henry, Virginia. The pilot boats of this period were steamers used to carry pilots to and from vessels. The date was c. 1910. This vessel could be the Virginia Pilot Association's pilot boat *Pilot*. Published by William J. O'Keefe & Company, the card was printed by the Albertype Company of Brooklyn, New York. (Courtesy of Edgar T. Brown.)

This penny postcard depicts the Life Savers' Drill Station, No. 1, Cape Henry, Virginia, also called the Cape Henry Life Saving Station No. 1, located near the lighthouses. Helen Cook wrote on the back, "The little boats sail just grand." Station surfmen had taken passengers out on one of the surfboats. Dated July 29, 1913, she continued, "the Captain took us up the lighthouse special." The postcard was sent to her husband, Leo Cook, at the Bureau of Lighthouses, Washington, D.C. (Courtesy of Edgar T. Brown.)

The Commonwealth of Virginia ceded its first acreage to the U.S. Army for a fort in March 1914. On July 24, 1916, the Army base was named Fort Story in honor of Maj. Gen. John P. Story, a pioneer in the development and application of artillery. The Army continued Atlantic Avenue from Eighty-ninth Street on the north end of the oceanfront, cutting between the old and new lighthouses, and eventually enjoining with Shore Drive at the convergence of Fort Story and First Landing/Seashore State Park. This photograph of Atlantic Avenue was taken in 1925. (Charles S. Borjes, photographer.)

On April 26, 1928, Governor Harry Flood Byrd of Virginia (above the pine boughs on the right) addressed the crowd at Cape Henry where the pilgrimage was made to pay annual tribute to the memory of the first Virginians to set foot there on April 26, 1607. (Photographer unknown.)

The pilgrimage ceremony had traditionally been atop the sand dune at the base of the old Cape Henry lighthouse, but in 1928, a natural amphitheater was dug out by the wind at the foot of the sand dune, so it was employed. Soldiers at Fort Story constructed a platform there, and raised a tall cross of Cape Henry pine before it. Around the edges of and in the "bowl," the crowd gathered. The April wind bit sharply and the sea rumbled nearby as the venerable old sentinel stood overlooking Governor Byrd and hundreds of people who braved the chill to attend the service. Tradition has it that in this spot, men from three tiny ships came on April 26, 321 years earlier, and raised a cross. (Photographer unknown.)

Storm action at Cape Henry necessitated the construction of berms constructed like levies to combat beach erosion. The stone cross, erected to symbolize the arrival of the first English settlers to the New World in 1607 and located near the old lighthouse, is visible to the right. The photograph was taken in November 1935 by Harold T. Cook of the Virginia Truck Experiment Station. The station developed the concept and oversaw construction of the berms. (Courtesy of the Hampton Roads Agricultural Research and Extension Center.)

The original Norwegian Lady remained a fixture on the oceanfront until 1953. Hurricanes and severe weather took their toll on the lady and she had to be removed to a city garage for storage. While in "storage," the neglected Norwegian Lady disintegrated; all that remains is a portion of her foot. A stone replica was erected at Twenty-fifth Street in 1962. The original Norwegian Lady was photographed for a postcard in front of Essex House, c. 1939. (Courtesy of Edgar T. Brown.)

Five

Jewel Resort of the Atlantic

"Out of the rolling ocean the crowd
came a drop gently to me . . .
I have travel'd a long way
merely to look on you to touch you."
—From *Out of the Rolling Ocean the Crowd*,
1865, 1881
Walt Whitman, American poet (1819–1892)

The Groves Bath House boasted the first saltwater swimming pool at Virginia Beach. Located south of the Seaside Park complex, which ran between Thirtieth and Thirty-third Streets, the Groves offered free dips in the pool to their patrons. Harry C. Mann took this picture about 1908. The Groves was a development conceived by James S. Groves, owner and president of the Virginia Beach Land Development Corporation. The Virginia Beach Land Development Corporation owned much of the property that encompassed early Virginia Beach and, as the price was right, gradually sold the land for development. The Groves family built a home in 1890 that sat at the corner of Twenty-fifth Street and Oceanfront. The family sold the house in the 1910s.

New Casino, Virginia Beach, Va.

The Virginia Beach Casino opened on June 1, 1912. The cost of the new park and casino was $120,000. The casino was built by Norfolk and Southern Railroad to bring people by rail car to the shore for recreation. The railroad made money from this venture faster than it could be counted. The park's famous Peacock Ballroom is to the far left, and the bathhouses are to the right in this c. 1912 postcard. The old dance trains would carry groups of young people to the casino for the evening. The trains were called the One-Step Special or the Two-Step Special, and this, of course, depended on the popular dance of the day. The grounds of the park and casino were connected by an exquisite system of sidewalks and landscaping. Partly destroyed by fire in 1956, a sizeable portion of Seaside Park was razed in 1982 to make way for new construction. The last of the legendary park met its end in 1986. (Courtesy of Edgar T. Brown.)

The Virginia Beach Casino had indoor and outdoor amusements, the Peacock Ballroom, a picnic pavilion, and a casino restaurant. Notice the roller coaster in the background. The roller coaster—called the Camel Back Coaster—a wooden "Skyscraper," and the Foolish House were added in 1913, about the date of the postcard. The half-mile track of the Camel Back Coaster was reportedly the highest and longest in the South. The casino was bought by a private investor and its name changed to Seaside Park. In 1926, a building was added to the park to house the merry-go-round and a few of the other concessions. (Courtesy of Edgar T. Brown.)

The Sam Simmons Orchestra was a rare treat for those who heard them play. This *c.* 1915 photograph shows the orchestra playing the famous Peacock Ballroom at Seaside Park. Sam Simmons is at the piano. The Peacock Ballroom was part of the original park complex. The most exciting period for the room was yet to come. Orchestras of national renown began to appear at the Peacock in the late 1910s and 1920s. By the 1930s, big band sounds reverberated through the Peacock. Tommy Dorsey played the Peacock for the first time in 1936, charging 10¢ a dance or three for 25¢.

Bathers enjoyed the open-air saltwater pool at the New Ocean Casino on July 4, 1926. The New Ocean Casino was built on the site of the old Princess Anne Hotel between Fourteenth and Sixteenth Streets. It opened in time for the 1925 tourist season and could accommodate 1,400 people in its bathhouse. The most unique feature of the casino was the pool shown here.

Walter C. Hagen (1892–1969), Gene "The Squire" Sarazen (1901–), and an amateur golfer named Forrester (from left to right in the foreground) participated in an October 1923 exhibition at Princess Anne Country Club, opened in 1920. The golf course was completed in 1921, and one of its earliest players was President Warren G. Harding in September of that year. Hagen was twenty-one years old when he won his first U.S. Open in 1914, and from the magic moment of that first U.S. Open, he would embark on a remarkable string of victories almost unparalleled in the history of golf. He was acknowledged as the best golfer of his day and voted one of the three best players of the first half of the twentieth century in the sportswriters' poll of 1950 along with Bobby Jones and Ben Hogan. Sarazen was a hard-working caddy before the First World War. He evolved from being a caddy to playing golf after the war, and by the time he was eighteen, he was considered a serious competitor. Gene Sarazen played in the U.S. Open in 1920 and 1921 and won the tournament in 1922 at the age of twenty. He won the Professional Golfers' Association (PGA) tournament in 1922 and 1923, beating Hagen in the final round. During the height of his career, Sarazen was a top money winner and popular showman. One of his enduring contributions to the game was his invention of the sand wedge in 1930.

A gentlemanly game of golf was being played on the miniature golf course at the Cavalier Hotel when this photograph was taken, *c*. 1927. (Photographer unknown.)

The saltwater swimming pool at Seaside Park was full of patrons on July 4, 1928. Located between Thirtieth and Thirty-third Streets at Virginia Beach, Seaside Park was originally constructed in 1906 by Norfolk and Southern Railroad and called the Virginia Beach Casino. The railroad brought passenger trains to the ends of the sidewalks leading up to the park. The park's saltwater pool is believed to have been the second of its kind introduced at the oceanfront.

On March 5, 1926, a name was chosen for what was to become the nation's leading hostelry for three decades—the Cavalier. Groundbreaking ceremonies were held on May 9, and thirteen months later, the seven-story Cavalier Hotel opened. The hotel had been constructed of cement-covered steel for fireproofing and was covered with over half a million bricks, the most ever used for one building in Virginia at that time. The Cavalier represented the epitomé of class and sophistication. Opening ceremonies were held over the week of April 4, 1927, and during the inaugural banquet on April 7, the Ben Bernie Band played. Colonel S.L. Slover,

president of the Cavalier Hotel Corporation, and Governor Harry Flood Byrd presided over the evening's festivities. A scrumptious banquet was served in seven courses, beginning with Canape Arlequin followed by Lynnhaven oysters, essence of celery, and mixed seafood Lillian. Spring chicken sauté Virginia and french green beans Suzette rounded out the main course, and then came salad Tidewater and strawberry plombiere with macaroons and ladyfingers. The photograph shown here was taken just after the Cavalier opened in 1927.

There were several unique features to the Cavalier Hotel that bear mention. The bathtubs of the hotel had a fourth handle for saltwater. People of the period thought saltwater had curative powers so, of course, the Cavalier catered to the times. The sinks had an ice-water faucet, but since the ability to pump cold water through the plumbing system was not what it is today, ice blocks were placed on the roof of the hotel in a large wooden tub. Force of gravity drew the ice water out of the tub through the pipes to each room. The lobby contained both a stock brokerage office with ticker tape directly from New York City and a radio station. WSEA was only the third radio station in the United States to broadcast coast to coast. Mayor Stockton Heth Tyler of Norfolk, standing in the studio of WSEA, became the first American to extend radio greetings to Charles A. Lindbergh as he passed old Cape Henry Lighthouse on his way to Washington, D.C., on June 10, 1927. Lindbergh was returning to America after his successful transatlantic solo flight from New York to Paris in competition for the Orteig Prize. The Sir Walter Raleigh Lounge of the hotel, pictured in 1927, was indicative of the luxurious appointments of the Cavalier.

The entrance to the lobby of the Cavalier had a 28-foot-in-diameter rotunda and ornamental plaster work on the ceiling copied from the entrance of the c. 1792 Moses Myers house on Freemason Street in downtown Norfolk. The picture was taken for a hotel promotional in 1927. (Photographer unknown.)

The saltwater pool at the Cavalier was a 75-foot-by-25-foot, heated, and chlorinated plunge for hotel patrons. The loggia is on the right in this 1927 photograph. Notice the original rattan and wicker furnishings along the rail of the loggia. Due to the military's base housing shortage for officers, the U.S. Navy took over the Cavalier on October 3, 1942, and while officers lived in the hotel, the Navy also opened a Fleet Service School to teach radar applications for the duration of World War II. The saltwater pool was drained and its basin used as a classroom to accommodate the overflow of students. (Photographer unknown.)

Children were provided with ample amusements at the Cavalier. Here, mothers give their youngsters a push on the swings in the children's playground. The photograph was taken by an unknown photographer in 1927.

Guests arriving at the Cavalier Hotel in their Rolls Royces, Pierce-Arrows, Chrysler Imperials, Cole Eight Nineties, Duesenbergs, and Essexes could rest assured their cars and drivers were pampered like royalty. The Cavalier had a dining room set aside just for chauffeurs. This photograph of the front entrance to the hotel was taken by an unnamed cameraman, c. 1928. By June 1928, Virginia Beach was experiencing its highest volume of Midwesterners to the shore because of the influx of Norfolk & Western Pullman cars running nonstop from Chicago to the depot at the Cavalier. The railroad had introduced its new gasoline-powered train *The Cavalier* about the time the Cavalier Hotel opened. The run from the Midwest to Virginia Beach became affectionately known as "The Cavalier to The Cavalier" train.

Actress Alice Joyce and her husband, James B. Regan Jr., visited the hotel in 1928 and are shown here posing in front of the Cavalier. Alice Joyce was famous in the era of silent films. Nicknamed "the Madonna of the Screen," Joyce was born on October 1, 1890, in Kansas City, Missouri. She appeared in eighty films between her premiere in *The Engineer's Sweetheart* in 1910 and *The Green Goddess* in 1930. Some of her film credits include lead roles in *Beau Geste* (1926), *The Vampire Trail* (1914), *The Hunchback* (1913), and *The Shadow* (1913). Alice Joyce died on October 9, 1955, of heart disease. Though Joyce was a popular and much-loved silent film star, her name, like so many of others of her time, is largely forgotten today and a substantial number of her films, particularly the early ones, are no longer in existence. (Photographer unknown.)

During Prohibition, the famous *New York World* writer, Franklin P. Adams, wrote in his column: "Prohibition is an awful flop. / We like it. / It can't stop what it's meant to stop, / We like it. / It's left a trail of graft and slime. / It's filled our land with vice and crime, / It can't prohibit worth a dime. / Nevertheless, we're for it." Adolph Coors, founder of the Colorado brewery bearing his name, might have enjoyed the oxymoron of the "noble experiment" had he lived to see it repealed in 1933 during Franklin D. Roosevelt's first-term as president of the United States. Coors plummeted to his death from the sixth floor of the Cavalier in June 1929. The circumstances of his death were suspicious, but the case was never officially attributed to foul play. Coors had turned to production of cement, malted milk, and pottery when Prohibition was ratified as the Eighteenth Amendment to the Constitution in 1919. This picture shows the two enclosed dining terraces on the south side of the hotel, 1927. (Photographer unknown.)

Mayor Stockton Heth Tyler presented the keys of the city of Norfolk to King Neptune at the opening of the Norfolk Regatta-Carnival, September 13, 1928. During the staging of sailboat races on the Lafayette River on the morning of September 14, King Neptune and the Queen of the Mardi Gras arrived at Naval Operating Base Norfolk where they were warmly received with military honors. Officers and enlisted men took part in a parade and review held in their honor, and various matches were conducted, including shooting events and aerial demonstrations. H.B. Carner, a local Buick automobile salesman, took first place in the flycasting contest. Lieutenant Alford J. "Al" Williams, the Navy's champion stunt flyer, had the honor of providing aerial thrills for the crowd that gathered at the naval base. (Photographer unknown.)

Father Neptune's parade float included a bevy of beautiful young ladies in 1928. The parade started the Norfolk Regatta-Carnival event. The first Norfolk Regatta-Carnival was held from August 18 to 21, 1926. During the 1926 event, which changed little from the one pictured here, King Neptune arrived on the Hague at 2:30 p.m. on August 18, accompanied by a military, civic, and fraternal parade. A dinner was held that evening at the Ocean View Hotel. Virginia Beach Night was held two days later and featured a carnival and Mardi Gras at the beach. The final day of the regatta-carnival focused on speedboat races. This was the biggest day of the festival for activities on the Eastern Branch of the Elizabeth River. Biscayne Babies, boats up from Florida, came for the 1926 festivities. Participants included hydroplanes of 510 and 151 Class as well. The final event was a dinner at the Ghent Club followed by fireworks. (Photographer unknown.)

Howard Keiffer, national junior trapshooting champion, gave an exhibition in the sunken gardens of the Cavalier Hotel as part of the Norfolk Regatta-Carnival on September 15, 1928. (Photographer unknown.)

The grounds of the Cavalier Hotel were designed by renowned landscape architect Charles Gillette of Richmond, Virginia. He consulted designs from plantations of Virginia at the time of the cavaliers such as Westover, Brandon, and Shirley to inspire the gardens of the hotel. Using native plantings, Gillette skillfully sculpted the massive hotel into the landscape. The sunken gardens, shown here on September 15, 1928, during the sports exhibition of the Norfolk Regatta-Carnival, was intended to be formal. It was planted on the south side of the hotel. Flowers from the sunken garden were used in the 195 guest rooms, 12 suites, dining room, and lobby. (Photographer unknown.)

H.L. Collier, of Dowagiac, Michigan, dubbed "Chief Dowagiac," was the nation's champion bait caster. He provided the crowd with elaborate exhibitions of his skill on September 15, 1928, rare treats to those who shared his passion for fishing.

Albert B. Schwarzkopf Jr. (pictured here), state model airplane flying champion, also gave an exhibition in the sunken gardens on September 15, 1928, much to the delight of the crowd. On September 14, model airplane races, which attracted wide attention, had been held in a hangar at Naval Air Station Hampton Roads. Tiny planes, operated with rubber bands, soared upward, circled among the beams until their power was exhausted, and then settled to the floor. Lieutenant Al Williams was one of the judges for the event. Young Smith McKann, of 215 East Thirty-ninth Street, was awarded first place in the indoor airplane races, and Albert Schwarzkopf Jr. of 609 Shirley Avenue, second place. More than a dozen youngsters competed for top honors. Following the indoor exhibitions, these youngsters moved into the outdoor phase of competition. Schwarzkopf took first place in the outdoor event, McKann second.

Captain Frank Winch (pictured here), former flycasting champion, gave an exhibition of his skill in the sunken gardens of the Cavalier Hotel on September 15, 1928, a fancy demonstration of casting characterized as "hurling a plug with the accuracy of rifle fire." Winch was not the only famous flycasting champion to appear at the sunken gardens that day. Also present was Fred G. Shaw, former international flycasting champion. Shaw demonstrated the ease with which he had captured world honors with the rod and reel in 1904. The sporting exhibition was part of the annual Norfolk Regatta-Carnival, earliest precursor of what evolved into the Neptune Festival. (Photographer unknown.)

Captain Winch shared the spotlight with his wife and her Llewellyn setter, Virginia Cavalier, on September 15, 1928, during a series of exhibitions in the sunken gardens of the Cavalier Hotel. Virginia Cavalier was christened and presented to the public during the show.

The *Miss RC²*, a Curtis DeLuxe outboard speedboat, was built by the Gas Engine & Boat Corporation of Norfolk, Virginia, and shipped to Germany to be raced on June 16, 1928, at Lake Templin, Pottsdam, Berlin, by Miss Helen Hentschel, outboard racing champion. The 12-and-1/2-foot outboard was the creation of the business owned by John Hughes Curtis, chairman of the Norfolk Regatta-Carnival Association. Helen Hentschel raced during the regatta-carnival, placing in two of the outboard races on the Eastern Branch of the Elizabeth River, September 14, 1928. (Photographer unknown.)

A party of four enjoys the afternoon on the putting green at the Cavalier, *c.* 1928.

Sporting her trademark "black helmet" haircut, Louise Brooks sips bottled water on the beach at the Cavalier Beach Club in 1929. Brooks was the epitomé of the Roaring '20s—a jazz baby, the symbol of anti-Prohibition America. The great William A. Wellman's film, *Beggars of Life* (with Wallace Berry and Richard Arlen, 1928), is Brooks' best American film. This down-to-earth vagabond melodrama in "Wild Bill" Wellman's repertoire is historically important as the first Paramount film to feature a talking sequence. Brooks plays a young girl who kills her stepfather in self-defense as he tries to rape her. She flees, dressed as a boy, with a hobo played by actor Richard Arlen. Brooks' character tries to reach Canada to evade arrest for murder. *Beggars for Life* is Brooks' first inroad into the area of sexual ambiguity which she would again explore in the film that established her as a great actress, G.W. Pabst's *Pandora's Box* (1929). Born in Cherryvale, Kansas, in 1906, Louise Brooks died on August 8, 1985, as Rochester, New York's most glamorous recluse. (Photographer unknown.)

A riding party was photographed departing the Cavalier c. 1929. The Cavalier maintained a string of Virginia and Kentucky thoroughbreds. Riders could select routes from 65 miles of bridle trails through pine forests, or water courses along country roads. The "Box Stall" on the knoll above the riding stables was a rustic retreat with a fireplace and restful furnishings. (Photographer unknown.)

This photograph was taken in May 1929 during the first horse show on the Cavalier Hotel's grounds. The horse show ring was located at the foot of the hotel terrace. The stable was operated by Colonel Boris La Boux. La Boux had been a cavalry officer in the Belorussian Army until he fled his homeland during the counterrevolution against communist rule that began in the summer of 1918 and did not end until 1922. The White counterrevolutionaries who challenged Red domination drew their strength from army officers like La Boux; the bourgeoisie; and political groups to the far right of Lenin's Socialist Revolutionaries. La Boux wisely departed the Soviet Union before the power struggle drew to its bloody close. (Photographer unknown.)

The Cavalier Beach Club opened on Memorial Day, 1929, to the sweet sounds of the McFarland Twins. The McFarland Twins had previously been saxophonists for the Fred Waring Orchestra. There were no other beach clubs in existence before the Cavalier Beach Club. From the day it opened until about 1959, the club was the biggest employer of big bands. Bing Crosby joined Paul Whiteman's orchestra in 1927 as a singer, and the same year, he partnered with Harry Barris to form the Rhythm Boys. The Rhythm Boys played the Cavalier Beach Club in 1930 just before they disbanded. The picture was taken in 1929. (Photographer unknown.)

The Cavalier Beach Club claimed only the sand in front of the club as patron-only territory. Taken on August 9, 1929, this picture shows the famous cabanas and colorful umbrellas that people came to associate exclusively with the hotel's beach club.

The saltwater pool at Seaside Park was a pleasurable respite from the sea, and always crowded. The boardwalk was obscured by the crowd in this photograph, taken June 23, 1929, by an unknown cameraman.

The Tom Thumb Miniature Golf Course, *c.* 1930, on the oceanfront was a popular amusement for vacationers and locals alike. (Photographer unknown.)

The slogan on the side of the airplane reads, "Virginia Beach, Year Round Play Ground," and this was as true then as it is now of the ocean resort. Charles S. Borjes took the photograph on August 11, 1930, at Grand Central Air Terminals field off Granby Street. The airplane was one of six that took off from the airfield on August 12 for a goodwill tour of Virginia with stops in key cities around the state. Lettering on the fuselages of the other airplanes read, "Spirit of Ocean View," "Norfolk-Portsmouth Chamber of Commerce," "Cities of Norfolk and Portsmouth," and "Grand Central Air Terminals." A plane from Newport News was added to the flight as well.

Britta Aspegren, daughter of Mr. and Mrs. Herman Aspegren of North Shore Point in Norfolk, took her first solo flight on Friday, August 29, 1930, after less than a month of flying instruction. Aspegren, taught by Dave Driskill, chief pilot at the Grand Central Air Terminals, was considered one of the most apt pupils of a class of forty students. She had less than ten hours in the air when she made her first solo in the aircraft that had been used two weeks earlier on a goodwill flight around Virginia. The aircraft reads, "Virginia Beach, Year Round Play Ground." (Photographer unknown.)

The Cavalier Hotel was one of the most photographed hotels in the United States in its heyday. The "Aristocrat of Virginia's Seashore" hosted the aristocracy of the nation, from seven U.S. presidents, including Calvin Coolidge, Herbert Hoover, Harry Truman, Dwight Eisenhower, John F. Kennedy, Lyndon B. Johnson, and Richard Nixon, to Hollywood stars and Broadway babies. F. Scott and Zelda Fitzgerald visited the Cavalier in the company of Joseph Hergesheimer in 1927. Judy Garland, Will Rogers, Ginger Rogers, Bette Davis, Jean Harlow, Betty Grable, and the opprobrious Fatty Arbuckle made their stays at the hotel something to remember. Mary Pickford and her husband, Buddy Rogers, visited in 1939. Hank Ketchum, his wife, Alice, and their famous son, Dennis, arrived at the hotel on July 1, 1953. Ketchum drew some of his popular "Dennis the Menace" comic strips based on the family's stay at the Cavalier. This Buffalo Bill look-alike with trusty steed posed with four lovely ladies at the Cavalier Beach Club in July 1932. (Photographer unknown.)

The four lovely ladies who posed with the Buffalo Bill look-alike staged several pictures for hotel promotionals. Here, they are shown walking through the archway on the brick path leading from the Cavalier to the beach club. The photograph was taken in July 1932. (Photographer unknown.)

A group of little girls attending Camp Owaisa at Chesapeake Beach watched Caroline Willis, Florence Siebert (counselor, left, in kneeling position), and Suzanne Taylor (right) demonstrate resuscitation. The date was July 28, 1932. Girls from seven to eleven years of age registered for the two-week program at Camp Owaisa through the Norfolk Young Women's Christian Association. Besides a regular schedule of swimming, dancing, games, and sports, there were activities such as rowing, crabbing, music, handicraft, and hiking. The girls even put on a play called *Snowdrop*. The title role was played by Constance Dean. Betty Funk was the queen; Katherine Fitzgerald, the prince; and Jane Skelton, the mirror. (Charles S. Borjes, photographer.)

Thousands of couples danced on the hardwood deck of the Cavalier Beach Club dance floor, seen here in 1934. The big bands that played the club during this era were led by some of the greatest musicians and composers of the twentieth century: Cab Calloway, Jimmy Dorsey, Duke Ellington, Benny Goodman, Hal Kemp, Johnny Long, Fats Waller, and Paul Whiteman. (Photographer unknown.)

Babe Zaharias (1914–1956), born Mildred Ella Didrikson, was an All-American basketball player in 1930 as a high school student. An exceptional all-around athlete, Didrikson won two gold medals in track and field events in the 1932 Olympic Games held in Los Angeles, California. She turned professional shortly thereafter. In 1935, Didrikson took up golf and, regaining her amateur status, she became the leading woman golfer in the United States. Three years later, Didrikson married wrestler George Zaharias. She was playing an exhibition at the Cavalier Country Club with Lew Worsham, Jack Hamilton ,and Walter Hagen Jr. on October 24, 1947, when this photograph was taken. (Charles S. Borjes, photographer.)

During 1947 alone, Babe Zaharias won seventeen straight golf titles, including the British Women's Amateur, a tournament that had never been won by an American. She became a professional golfer and continued her winning streak. She was voted the most outstanding woman athlete of the century in an Associated Press poll in 1949. Zaharias died of cancer in 1956, but not before publishing her autobiography, *This Life I've Led*, in 1955. Babe Zaharias was photographed in the Cavalier course clubhouse on October 25, 1947, with a friend. (Charles S. Borjes, photographer.)

These "Dianas of the Beach" were taking archery lessons at the Cavalier Beach Club during the last week of July 1932. The club enjoyed a successful summer in 1932, but in August and September 1933, it sustained serious damage from devastating hurricanes. The club was rebuilt quickly and business resumed as usual. (Photographer unknown.)

Six
Inland Waters

"Thou in thy narrow banks art pent:
The stream I love unbounded goes
Through flood and sea and firmament;
Through light, through life, it forward flows."
—From *Two Rivers*, 1856, 1867
Ralph Waldo Emerson, American poet
(1803–1882)

From sea and endless dunes, to advancing sand and desert, in wilderness and marsh, the Cape Henry area of Virginia Beach had all the attributes of a wilderness oasis. Harry C. Mann preserved the incomparable marsh areas of Cape Henry with his series of photographs taken *c.* 1910. Lush and beautiful, these marshes speak well to the Chinese proverb, "One seeing is worth a hundred Tellings."

Lake Holly, photographed by an unknown cameraman in 1896, was located about two blocks inland from the Virginia Beach shoreline. The lake was a prime breeder of mosquitoes, those pesky summertime insects who became the bane of Virginia Beach resort developers anxious to draw customers to the oceanfront. Bernard P. Holland conceived of an idea he called "the Flume," a device that transferred saltwater by wave action into Lake Holly, thus making the lake saltwater as well. Work on the Flume was completed in September 1890. This picture was taken after the Flume had begun operation. The Flume itself would have met its end over time as silt deposited in the tube, but the hurricanes of 1933 ripped the structure apart.

Oysters could be found in plentiful numbers in the waters of the Chesapeake Bay, in Hampton Roads, the York and James Rivers, off Lynnhaven Inlet, Ocean View, and in other favorable locations within a short distance of Norfolk. Workers at Hopkins Fish & Oyster Company posed for this photograph in front of a large shell pile in Atlantic City in 1910. In late fall and early winter, small boats could be seen in the Lynnhaven River tonging for seed oysters which were then bought by the packers from the tongers working the rocks for planting in packers' private beds. When grown to marketable size, which took anywhere from two to four years, the oysters were dredged up and taken to the packing houses. (Photographer unknown.)

The Roper Cedar Mill, c. 1907, was located in Lower Norfolk County, but it is a good example of the milling operations that were once situated along the back inlets and bays of Virginia Beach and Cape Henry. These mills were placed in areas with rich timber stands of cedar and pine.

A site off the Little Creek Reservoir and Norfolk and Southern Railroad right-of-way was selected by the State Agricultural Board in August 1906 as a site for agricultural experimentation; such a facility was much-needed. After the Civil War, Virginia vegetable growers enjoyed particularly good market advantages, shipping their goods easily to large markets in the North. There was little competition from anyone else in the South. While business was booming, Virginia's soil could not continue to undergo hard use, and farmers had begun to notice an increase in crop disease and insect infestations. Southern Produce Company, an organization of truck crop growers and market gardeners in the Norfolk area, took the first steps toward establishing a vegetable research center. For the first time in U.S. history, there was a facility devoted to farming experimentation, including soil and plant testing, cultivation methods, and fertilizer development. The center was called the Virginia Truck Experiment Station from 1907 to 1967. The barn and shack in this photograph were on the land when it was taken over by the state in 1907. The area chosen for the Virginia Truck Experiment Station was ideal for practical reasons. The station bordered the Norfolk and Southern track connecting Norfolk and its valuable shipping facilities to Virginia Beach and Princess Anne County truck farmers. The railroad line passing the station was the same track that also enjoined the resort end of the beach to its tourist population. The line was heavily used by both passenger excursion trains and truck farmers moving their crops to market. (Courtesy of the Hampton Roads Agricultural Research and Extension Center.)

The Virginia Truck Experiment Station was also once surrounded by potato fields. The barn found on the property when the state took over the land may have been used as a storage point for potatoes before they were loaded on the train headed for Norfolk. The earliest known drawing of the potato (shown here), *Solanum tuberosum*, was rendered in 1588, and published in 1601 by Carolus Clusius. (Courtesy of the Hampton Roads Agricultural Research and Extension Center.)

The first director of the Virginia Truck Experiment Station, Thomas C. Johnson, M.A. (pictured here from an oil-on-canvas portrait), assumed his duties in 1907 and worked at the station until his death in 1932. Dr. Howard H. Zimmerly succeeded Johnson and served until his death in 1944. The station became a separate state agency on March 1, 1920, and in 1985, Virginia Polytechnic Institute and State University assumed management of the facility and renamed it the Hampton Roads Agricultural Research and Extension Center. (Courtesy of the Hampton Roads Agricultural Research and Extension Center.)

The Virginia Truck Experiment Station staff members were photographed on the steps of the director's house during the summer of 1909. Pictured from left to right are as follows: Joseph Milstead of the U.S. Department of Agriculture (USDA); C.S. Heller; Miss Monnie Leatherbury, secretary; Thomas C. Johnson, director; and Alfred Orcutt, also with the USDA. The USDA was a partner in the station's development from the outset. Over the years, the staff of the station would include some of the nation's leading agricultural scientists.

With their mandate in hand and a site preselected by the state, local growers purchased 58.8 acres of neglected, weed-infested land 6 miles northeast of downtown Norfolk at Diamond Springs, Princess Anne County, on February 25, 1907. The barn in this photograph, taken in 1908, was the first of its type of building to be constructed by the Virginia Truck Experiment Station on the property. It was used for housing mules and farming equipment. The growers subsequently acquired four smaller tracts that almost doubled the available area for experimentation. (Both photographs on this page courtesy of the Hampton Roads Agricultural Research and Extension Center.)

Several buildings were constructed on the site of the Virginia Truck Experiment Station between 1908 and 1911. The director's residence (left), barn and water tower (center), and office and laboratory building were constructed in 1908. The greenhouse (right) was built in 1911. The photograph was taken on May 14, 1914.

The directors of the Southern Produce Company were photographed on the porch of the director's residence at the Virginia Truck Experiment Station in 1913. Their period of individual service on the station's board of directors is bracketed behind their names. From left to right, they are as follows: (front row) W.J. Heard; J.E. "Ed" Ames; Ed Holland; John T. Griffin (1907–1920); Henry Kirn (president of Southern Produce Company); C.W. Coleman; H.J. Robertson; John G. Eberwine (1920–1924); and Lem Lamb; (back row) Burt C. Haines (1945–1948); Daniel W. Lindsey (1920–1945); Thomas C. Johnson (director, 1907–1932); Henry C. Cooper; Lindsey Sylvester; W.B. Carney (1907–1920); Larenzo A. Deans; T.W. Butt; T.G. Barlow; and John Perrott. The station's original governing board consisted of six members, two of whom were named from the Southern Produce Company. The company ceased operation in 1946, and its place on the board was taken by the Association of Virginia Potato Growers by an act of the General Assembly. (Both photographs on this page courtesy of the Hampton Roads Agricultural Research and Extension Center.)

Real beauty is found when one comes upon a trail or untracked way through a forest and that path breaks clear to blue, sparkling, yet mysterious, waters beneath a dune far inland. The image (top, opposite page) was part of Long Creek, a narrow, winding course to Broad Bay, c. 1910. White Hill, one of only many mounds of sand along White Hill Lake, otherwise known as Broad Bay, is depicted in the bottom image on the opposite page. Here, one was far from the sea and the world. The above image is also of Broad Bay. While in the forest, a frog croaks, or a whippoorwill cries his mournful plaint, or a twig crackles underfoot; silence otherwise quickly overtakes you. Only the muffled brushing of the sand and the quiet whisper of little waves slapping to and fro along the inner bay could pull one toward the water. (Harry C. Mann, photographer.)

Dr. John Miller Masury, son of a wealthy New York paint and oil manufacturer and heir to a fortune, came to Virginia Beach in November 1905 to purchase property for a summer home from Mrs. S.K. Uber. Mrs. Uber's property was 130 acres of prime waterfront land half a mile's walk from the lakeshore to oceanfront. Masury erected a twenty-five-room mansion built of gray stone from Scotland in 1908. Masury dubbed his home "Lakeside" for its location on Crystal Lake. The house was impressive and included a ballroom, pipe organ, elevator, and cedar boardwalk from the house to oceanfront. The electric lights in the house drew their power from Masury's private electric plant. This plant provided electricity to his boardwalk and beach cottage as well as an electric train that ran along Atlantic Avenue. For a time, Lakeside was the only house between Thirty-first Street and Cape Henry. During the 1930s, Lakeside was converted to the Crystal Club, a casino and nightclub, but after World War II, it reverted back to a home. The photograph was taken c. 1915. Crystal Lake may have been an accessible inlet to the ocean according to maps of the Spanish expedition of 1570. The Spanish documented access points to the Atlantic in the Cape Henry and Virginia Beach area and noted several inlets that are now landlocked.

The location of the mounds in this photograph is believed to be near Lake Joyce where the Chesokoiack or Chesapean Indians were active. The Chesapeans were very knowledgeable of the rivers and inland waters of the lower Chesapeake Bay and most especially the reaches of what would eventually be called Cape Henry and Lynnhaven. A peaceful and intelligent people, the Chesapeans found peace with the Earth and communed with it. Chesapean tribal leadership was usurped by Powhatan in 1595. He killed off the adult-male members of the Chesapean tribe, letting only the women, children, and royal family live. Powhatan had already conquered most of the tribes from the James River to the Potomac River, incorporating them into his confederacy, at the time he ventured south and ravaged the Chesapeans. The photograph was taken in 1930, and the mounds were already becoming overgrown with scrub pines and mixed vegetation. Archaeologist Floyd Painter found that the Lake Joyce area off Chesapeake Beach was almost precisely the site of the Chesapean village known as Apasus. It is believed that the site's ancient history, rooted in the Apasus culture, would make it the oldest continuously occupied site since the English settled at Jamestown in 1607.

Soon after its 1927 opening, the Cavalier Hotel promised its patrons that it would be building a country club that provided golf and trapshooting courses. In the interim, the hotel made arrangements with Princess Anne Country Club management to use their golf course. The Cavalier Country Club, shown here under construction in June 1930, is situated at the apex of Linkhorn Bay and Little Neck Creek on a finger of land known as Bird Neck Point. Richard Crane, owner of Westover plantation in Charles City County and a former diplomat, was in the process of developing Bird Neck Point when the ownership of the Cavalier Hotel approached him with idea of building a first-class golf course and country club on the property. Crane agreed and donated the land to the hotel for that purpose. The club was completed shortly after this photograph was taken. It became famous for its golf course, trapshooting facilities, and horseback riding. Sam Snead won the Virginia Open on the Cavalier Country Club's golf course in 1935, the same year the Cavalier Hotel and its satellite facilities were named Virginia Beach's largest industry. The U.S. Navy took over the club during World War II as an officers' club for the Fleet Service School, a radar training program, located at the Cavalier Hotel. In 1946, the club added piers and did away with the traps along the water's edge. The name was subsequently changed to the Cavalier Yacht and Country Club. When the stables were replaced by tennis courts and a swimming pool, the name was appropriately changed to the Cavalier Golf and Yacht Club. (Photographer unknown.)

Patrons of the Cavalier Hotel took advantage of hunting in Back Bay and Currituck, North Carolina. The duck hunters depicted in this image were on Back Bay when an unknown photographer took their picture in 1930. Upon returning to the hotel from a hunting excursion, the Cavalier Hunt Room, a private men's club for hunters, was open for their use. Guests' dogs could be kept on the hotel grounds, and fish caught and game killed during the hunt taken to the kitchen and prepared for dinner.

Members of the Virginia Commission on Game and Inland Fisheries were on a tour of the commonwealth to survey the game situation when they stopped off at the Cavalier Country Club on October 11, 1930, as special guests of the Cavalier Gun Club and the Norfolk Chapter of the Izaak Walton League at an oyster roast followed by trapshooting. Those in the photograph (from left to right) were L.W. Tyus, fiscal secretary of the commission; B.W. Stras, Tazewell; M.D. Hart, secretary, Richmond; Major A. Willis Robertson, chairman, Lexington; Richard Crane, Westover; S.R. Goodloe, Afton; and C.H. Nolting, Louisa. The commissioners' visit to Norfolk was the last stop on the tour. Major Robertson remarked of Hampton Roads, "Residents of this section cannot possibly realize how fortunate they are until they see the seared fields of the Valley, the dried up trout streams and the burned-over forest areas where deer have been killed or routed from their native heath, and where fine wild turkey nests are in ruins." (Charles S. Borjes, photographer.)

The trapshooting courses at the Cavalier Country Club were some of the finest in Virginia. The picture shown here was taken in 1930. (Photographer unknown.)

A few local boys enjoy a dip at Diamond Springs on May 23, 1947. The Diamond Springs area was originally part of a place called Middletown in the nineteenth century. The water in this Diamond Springs happened to be the irrigation pond of the agricultural research and extension service operated by Virginia Polytechnic Institute and State University. (Charles S. Borjes, photographer.)

Seven

Along the Boardwalk

"I pace the sounding sea-beach and behold
   How the voluminous billows roll and run,
   Upheaving and subsiding, while the sun
   Shines through their sheeted emerald far unrolled,
And the ninth wave, slow gathering fold by fold
      All its loose-flowing garments into one,
   Plunges upon the shore, and floods the dun
   Pale reach of sands, and changes them to gold."
      —From *Milton*, 1873, 1875
         Henry Wadsworth Longfellow, American poet
         (1807–1882)

Crowds enjoyed the new promenade at Virginia Beach in this *c.* 1929 photo. The new concrete promenade was less than a year old when this picture was taken by an unknown photographer. The roped-off area in the surf to the right was intended for children and adults with little to no experience swimming. A natural "wading pool" of sorts, this area was certainly not a bad idea.

The original wooden boardwalk was built in 1888, originating at the old Princess Anne Hotel and running south along the ocean between Twelfth to Sixteenth Streets. This boardwalk was razed by the hotel fire that swept along the oceanfront in 1907, and it was not until 1926 that work was begun on a new concrete promenade. Though this new structure was made of concrete, the term "boardwalk" stuck. The initial phase of the concrete promenade was completed in 1927. A committed group of beach property owners sought to extend the new promenade from Thirty-fifth Street to Fiftieth Street. These property owners formed the Virginia Beach Walkway Corporation. After a $250,000 bond issue was voted and approved, construction took place in the early months of 1928. The new portion of the promenade was christened and opened to the public on May 26 (shown here). A ribbon-cutting ceremony to officially permit the first traffic on the ocean promenade occurred the same day. A band played as two young ladies opened the gates for Norfolk's finest on motorcycles. It was not until 1938 and 1939 that wooden bulkheads were added to the concrete portion of the walkway and the boardwalk extended to the Cavalier Hotel.

Early risers could walk south beyond the end of the promenade at Virginia Beach in the early morning hours and watch Stormont fishing boats setting out for their pound nets and returning with their catch. Trawlers could also be seen leaving Lynnhaven Inlet for their fishing grounds 40 to 50 miles offshore. Fishermen would select their best food fish and sell them to customers off the boat. The transaction taking place in this *c.* 1930 picture was commonplace many years ago. (Photographer unknown.)

Taken *c.* 1930 by an unknown photographer, this picture of a happy young man and his catch is reminiscent of a line from *The Song of the Fishes*: "Up jumped the fisherman, his face all a-grin, / And with his big net he scooped them all in!"

105

One of the first privately-owned airships of its kind, the Goodyear NC-18A *Enna Jettick*, flew over the Virginia Beach oceanfront on July 26, 1931, and landed on the beach for the crowds to look and, if their nerves allowed, get a ride. The *Enna Jettick*, built by Goodyear's Akron plant, was 138 feet long, 38 feet in diameter, and filled with non-flammable helium gas. It was quite rare for Goodyear not to have operated the *Enna Jettick*. Upon completion of construction at Akron in 1930, the airship had been designated the NC-13A *Neponset*. The *Neponset* was renamed the NC-18A *Enna Jettick* in 1931 after sale to Enna Jettick Shoes, a national chain. The airship was on a tour of the United States for the company. She was deflated in 1932 and later dismantled. Norfolk had an Enna Jettick Boot Shop at 405 Granby Street, and Portsmouth had a store at 700 High Street.

This picture of a typical day at the beach, *c.* 1935, shows a section of the famous promenade. Notice the unique patterned umbrellas dotting the beach.

Eight
A Day on the Beach

"The child and the ocean still smile on each other."
—From *A Vision of the Sea*, 1820
Percy Bysshe Shelley, English poet
(1792–1822)

A group of young people are enjoying a day at the beach along the Cottage Line on March 7, 1896. Those in the picture include Thomas Turner, Cornelia Tucker, I.T. Walke, and Jenny Drewry.

People would come to Sand Hill at Cape Henry, climb to the top, picnic, and enjoy the view from atop what, at that time, was the second largest dune at the beach. In the image shown here, taken c. 1905, beachgoers climbed past the tops of dead trees that protruded from the steep slope, past the matted bulwark of live ones at the bottom, and all the vegetation that held tenuously to the incline. (Photographer unknown.)

Bathers enjoy the waters off Virginia Beach c. 1908. (Harry C. Mann, photographer.)

The long coastline of Virginia Beach and Cape Henry was characterized by its song of loneliness and the beauty of its tide-swept sands. In early May, bathers began to return to the beach, and the solitude of its shores quickly filled with the laughter of children and the banter of young people frolicking in the surf. Lifelines were erected along the beach to assist inexperienced swimmers and young children caught by surprise in the surf. The surf looked particularly inviting the day the picture was taken in 1908. Each wave created a new picture. Beyond the line of surf, beachgoers of this period, in particular, remembered seeing schools of dolphins. This Harry C. Mann image was printed backwards.

The handstand trick seemed to remain a popular feat of showmanship for young men visiting the beach. Harry C. Mann took this picture in 1908.

Ladies and gentlemen dressed in their finest apparel to visit the beach on a Sunday afternoon, while others came well prepared in the latest swimsuit fashion to take a dip in the ocean. Harry

C. Mann captured this weekend ritual with his camera, looking through the bathhouse entrance at Seaside Park, *c.* 1908. Notice the lovely matching hats of the ladies on the right.

Harry C. Mann photographed the entrance to the beach from the bathhouses at Seaside Park, c. 1910. The "Slide for Life" was billed as a thrilling and exciting ride. It required slipping into a harness and sliding down the wire into the surf. The cost was one ride for a nickel or six rides for a quarter.

Harry C. Mann photographed beachgoers over several years. This photograph was thought to have been taken about 1912. The Flume is visible to the upper right of the picture. The boardwalk offered many diversions for visitors, including canoes, sailboats, and saltwater pools. Canoers are shown in the water, also to the right side of the image.

Beauty contestants competed in the first Miss Virginia pageant ever held in the state, and the first to take place at Virginia Beach, in 1926. The competition was staged at Seaside Park. One of these bathing beauties was chosen as Miss Virginia, and went on to compete in the Miss America pageant that year. She lost to Norma Smallwood of Tulsa, Oklahoma, who won the crown. The national competition had only been in business since 1921. Virginia has only had one winner in the history of the Miss America pageants. Kylene Barker won in 1979. (Photographer unknown.)

Miss Virginia pageant contestants posed with a lifeguard on the beach near Seaside Park. From this picture, one can see that lifeguards lead such hard lives. The picture was taken in 1926 by an unknown photographer.

These bathing beauties, contestants in the Miss Virginia pageant of 1926, are modeling the best of the season's swimwear at Virginia Beach. (Photographer unknown.)

Virginia Beach played host to some thirty thousand people on July 4, 1928, the largest crowd of beachgoers recorded in the resort's history up to that time. Young and old, grandmothers and grandfathers, and even infants in arms made up the crowd that thronged the sands of Virginia Beach. During the early evening, a beautiful display of fireworks was set off in front of the cottages and hotels that lined the promenade, lending a true Fourth of July atmosphere to the occasion, and at 10:30, another display was sent up from the Cavalier Hotel. (Photographer unknown.)

Bathers test the waters during a glorious Fourth of July at Virginia Beach. The year was 1928, and despite the largest crowd in its history, there were no serious accidents to mar the pleasure of the day. A physician in Virginia Beach declared that he had fewer calls on July 4, 1928, than on any Fourth of July in his recollection. (Photographer unknown.)

On July 4, 1929, a happy couple posed for a friend at Virginia Beach. (Photographer unknown.)

The dog days of summer drew these children into the water at Virginia Beach, c. 1929. The little girl in the foreground seems to be enjoying herself while riding the safety ropes as the waves broke on the shore. (Photographer unknown.)

Beachgoers enjoy the sun and surf of Virginia Beach, c. 1932. (Photographer unknown.)

A day on the beach turned very exciting on April 26, 1930, when the Goodyear airship *Vigilant*, NC-11A, of St. Petersburg, Florida, landed in the surf. The *Vigilant*, part of Goodyear's advertising fleet, was built in 1929. The date of the airship envelope's deflation is unknown, but it is suspected to be about 1931. The *Vigilant* had come to Virginia Beach to participate in the Cape Henry Day celebration.

This scene, photographed by an unknown photographer on the private beach of the Cavalier Beach Club, was taken about 1932. The men on horseback came down the hill from the Cavalier Hotel stables and are headed up the beach. There are only men in the photograph, and though details are not known, the explanation was that there was a party taking place on the beach that day from one or several of the cabanas. In any case, the composition of the photograph demonstrates how diverse, even in the 1930s, beach dress could be—anything from a business suit and military uniform to bathing suit were acceptable.

A daredevil pilot landed his aircraft on the beach, June 23, 1935. It was not unusual for stunt flyers to pull a feat like landing on a beach and offering rides to curious onlookers. This aircraft has a fancy red-and-white paint scheme. (Charles S. Borjes, photographer.)

The daughter of a U.S. senator and the son of another senator were married quietly on July 4, 1934, at the Cavalier Hotel. The bride, Frances Jackson Reynolds, daughter of Sen. Robert R. Reynolds of Asheville, North Carolina, and the bridegroom, Lieutenant LeBaron Carlton Colt of the U.S. Army, a native of New Hampshire, but stationed at Windsor, North Carolina, were married by the Reverend Benjamin Boyd Bland of the Methodist church shortly before noon. They were photographed by Charles S. Borjes at the Cavalier Beach Club later that afternoon, but both evaded questions from reporters pertaining to their acquaintance and subsequent marriage. The Colts spent time in the company of friends during their stay at the Cavalier Hotel, and from reporters' observations, made every effort to keep to themselves. The elopement of these children of famous fathers made the press diligently pursue the couple.

A dozen young women posed playfully in the surf of Virginia Beach in 1960. Does anyone look familiar? (Photographer unknown.)

Nine

Big Bands, World War, and Unforgettable Memories

Then, then, ye ocean-warriors!
    Our song and feast shall flow
To the fame of your name,
    When the storm has ceased to blow!
When the fiery fight is heard no more,
    And the storm has ceased to blow."
        —From *Ye Mariners of England*, 1801
        Thomas Campbell, English poet (1775–1834)

Two young women sport the latest in beach attire and sea life. The woman on the right is gingerly holding onto an expired sand crab, c. 1944. (Photographer unknown.)

The Cavalier was the largest hirer of big bands in the world in the 1930s, 1940s, and 1950s. The biggest names in the business took the bandstand facing the Atlantic Ocean, including Tommy Dorsey, Jimmy Dorsey, Glenn Miller, Harry James, Benny Goodman, Xavier Cugat, Cab Calloway, Lawrence Welk, Bing Crosby, Guy Lombardo, Judy Garland, Johnny Long, and the incomparable Frank Sinatra. They all played the Cavalier Beach Club and each graced its stage with their unforgettable music and memories. Young couples enjoyed the sounds of big bands and danced the afternoon and evening away. This picture was taken sometime during the summer of 1941, and it is typical of the crowds that filled the dance floor every season from Memorial Day to Labor Day. The Cavalier Beach Club continued to flourish after the start of World War II. By October 3, 1942, the federal government had informed the Cavalier's management that the Navy required the use of its hotel on the hill to operate a radar training school. (Photographer unknown.)

The war period had its share of dreadful uncertainties, and with its end, carefree days at the beach returned. Here, a couple of daring young men delight their female companions in front of the cabanas at the Cavalier Beach Club with a display of strength and balance, c. 1947. There were over one hundred of these cabanas in two wooden tiers along the stretch of beach off the club. The ones closest to the beach, such as those shown here, were most prized. (Photographer unknown.)

A day of fun in the sun has left this young woman soundly asleep on the beach, c. 1947. (Photographer unknown.)

TREASURE OF THE CAVALIER

Carlos Wilson came to work at the Cavalier Hotel as a busboy in 1937. After sixty years of working at the hotel and having never missed a day of work, he is director of guest services at the new Cavalier and has no plans for retirement. Though he would take a week's vacation at Christmas and some time off after his wife passed away, Wilson has entered the doors of the Cavalier every day with a smile on his face and a kind word for its patrons. He has made conversation with presidents of the United States and movie stars, and listened to the greatest big bands in history under the stars at the Cavalier Beach Club. When asked his favorite remembrance of the big bands, Wilson replied, "Mr. Glenn Miller." As the story goes, "Mr. Miller was playing up on the stage of the beach club one beautiful summer night, and in those days you had to be a member of the club or a hotel guest to get in, well, there were all these kids hooping and hollering down on the beach to the sweet sounds of the music. You know what he did? Mr. Miller took that horn of his and stepped off the stage and parted the crowd on the dance floor as he walked down to the beach in the middle of all those kids. He kept playing the whole time. You should've seen those people on the dance floor in their evening gowns and tuxedos follow him down to the beach. The men were rolling up their pants legs and the ladies taking off their shoes. Glenn Miller had as much feeling for the nonpaying customers as the paying ones. That was the kind of man he was. The night was unforgettable." In those days, one big band would play the Cavalier for up to a week at a time while another would be down at the Surf Club or Ocean View. Wilson remarked that he was so young when he began working at the hotel that when someone asked him to serve tea at the Cavalier Beach Club's famous tea dances, he thought you actually served tea. "I made tea, but they wanted whiskey. Tea looked like whiskey in the cup until they took a sip." The best night of his life was the evening Japan capitulated in World War II. He made $600 in one night because naval officers at the beach club went wild with excitement and kept giving him money. "If I'd been a drinking man, I would've had a drink that night. I just held on to my money and caught the trolley home."

The annual pilgrimage to Cape Henry, marking the 338th anniversary of the first landing by permanent English colonists, took on special meaning on April 26, 1945. Convalescent soldiers formed a large part of the audience which heard addresses by the governor of Virginia and the Right Reverend William A. Brown, D.D., bishop of southern Virginia. This was the first time since the United States entered World War II that the pilgrims made their way to Cape Henry. (Charles S. Borjes, photographer.)

Ten

Storm-tossed Shores And a New Virginia Beach Resort

"Often I think of the beautiful town
That is seated by the sea;
Often in thought go up and down
The pleasant streets of that dear old town,
And my youth comes back to me."
—From *My Lost Youth*, 1855
Henry Wadsworth Longfellow, American poet
(1807–1882)

The annual Shriners Parade at the oceanfront was a particular cause for celebration on September 11, 1954. Hurricane Edna had threatened to spoil the activities of the Mid-Atlantic Shrine Convention, but it dissipated and the Shriners' noisy parade made its way down Atlantic Avenue. Several thousand Shriners from sixteen Eastern temples exhibited their traditional enthusiasm, stretching the parade at one point from its convention headquarters at the Cavalier into the heart of the loop at the opposite end of Atlantic. Shriners dressed as clowns, and policemen tossed candy to children in the crowd. Firecrackers exploded in the street, and on the west side of Thirty-ninth Street, a Shrine unit from Norfolk's Khedive Temple put on an impromptu Dixieland concert. The convention climaxed with a fireworks display and dances at the Cavalier Beach and Cabana Club and the Surf Beach Club, and a street dance at Twenty-second Street. (Jim Mays, photographer.)

This photograph by R.K.T. Larson shows Rudee Inlet as it looked in 1952. The deteriorating remnants of the old rail bridge to Cape Henry is in the foreground. The rail bridge was later torn down because it had become as much a hazard to water navigation as an eyesore. The concrete remains of the concrete bridge over the inlet were washed away by the hurricanes of 1933 and subsequent storm action. In 1952, Virginia Beach had become independent of Princess Anne County.

The Ash Wednesday storm of March 7, 1962, began two days earlier and moved across Virginia from the mountains at the far western tip of the state. Snow clouds traveled eastward, covering much of the state with wet, heavy snow. By the time it reached the coast, the storm had transformed into something much more devastating to residents of Virginia's shores. The coastal areas of Virginia were hit by a violent nor'easter the morning of the seventh. Twenty- to thirty-foot waves and tides recorded at over 7 feet eroded the beach and destroyed significant portions of the boardwalk (shown here). (Photographer unknown.)

These photographs show the extent of damage to beach homes between Forty-sixth and Forty-seventh Streets after the ocean had begun receding. There were 340 homes in Virginia Beach damaged or destroyed on March 7, 1962, in addition to several business establishments, hotels, and recreational facilities along the oceanfront. In the foreground of the bottom photograph is a portion of the wreck of the Norwegian bark *Dictator*, exposed by the storm. (Photographer unknown.)

The Virginia Beach oceanfront had grown from a strip of quaint summer cottages and palatial hostelries, parks, and casinos to an architecturally diverse and expansive array of chain hotels and seaside motels when this picture was taken c. 1960. Few reminders of the past were still standing as old made way for new.

BIRTH OF THE CITY

The first annexation of part of Princess Anne County by the future city of Virginia Beach had its origins in 1923 with the acquisition of a section of the county by the town of Virginia Beach. The town entered a water agreement with the city of Norfolk in 1924, and two years later, the wooden boardwalk was replaced by a concrete promenade. The city of Norfolk annexed 13.5 square miles of the county on January 1, 1959, and sensing more annexation to come, the city of Virginia Beach and Princess Anne County joined together in a campaign to halt further annexations. A referendum was held on January 4, 1962, and voters approved a consolidation agreement by a five-to-one margin. The merger became effective January 1, 1963, and the city of Virginia Beach was truly born. Though the city of Virginia Beach is today more than a resort area with a land area of 310 square miles, the resort has placed the city's name on maps across the country.